COOKING
FOR THE HOLIDAYS

**DO NOT REMOVE
CARDS FROM POCKET**

Also by the author:

Easy Livin' Microwave Cooking

EASY LIVIN' MICROWAVE COOKING

FOR THE HOLIDAYS

BY KAREN KANGAS DWYER

• ST. MARTIN'S PRESS NEW YORK •

Library of Congress Cataloging-in-Publication Data
Dwyer, Karen.
    Easy livin' microwave cooking for the holidays / Karen Kangas Dwyer.
      p. cm.
    ISBN 0–312–03480–6
    1. Microwave cookery. 2. Holiday cookery. I. Title. II Title:
Easy living microwave cooking for the holidays.
TX832.D984 1989
641.5′8–dc20   89–34852

Second Edition

10 9 8 7 6 5 4 3 2 1

DEDICATION

———— · ✳ · ————

I dedicate this book to all those who, like myself, love good old-fashioned holiday foods yet find their time to produce family favorites so limited.

This book is my attempt to make holiday cooking ever so easy and enjoyable with the help of the microwave oven.

I also dedicate this book to Billie Oakley, KMA morning radio show host, in Shenandoah, Iowa, and all of the wonderful KMA audience who daily share such a love for life, nostalgia, and good old-fashioned cooking. Many of these recipes are adaptations or inspirations "called in" from the listeners.

Last of all, I dedicate this book to my husband, Larry, for whose help and encouragement I am always thankful.

CONTENTS

· ❄ ·

INTRODUCTION

· ❄ ·

Nothing speaks of nostalgia and the holidays like the aroma and taste of home-cooked candies, cakes, breads, and special family dinners. Yet as the holidays approach, increased activities and busy schedules often inhibit the time available to make these favorite family treats.

The microwave oven makes it easy to enjoy traditional foods in the midst of a limited time schedule.

In this book you will find cherished holiday recipes from the past and the present, all adapted to be used with this new and wonderful time-saver, the microwave oven.

Christmas, New Year's Day, Easter, Independence Day, Labor Day, and Thanksgiving can all be celebrated with your favorite foods. Holiday cooking may become so easy that any day can be a holiday with the microwave oven!

Included also are the basics of microwaving and many tips on how to convert your favorite conventional recipes to microwave recipes. So . . . ENJOY! ENJOY! ENJOY!

HAPPY HOLIDAY MICROWAVING TO YOU ALL.

Karen

ANSWERS TO BASIC MICROWAVE QUESTIONS

· ❄ ·

WHAT ARE MICROWAVES AND HOW DOES THE MICROWAVE OVEN WORK?

Microwaves are simply electromagnetic waves that penetrate food and cause the liquid molecules in the food to vibrate approximately two and one-half billion times per second. The vibrating molecules in the food create friction. The friction produces heat that, in turn, causes the food to actually cook itself.

Microwaves are produced in the same way in every micro-wave oven.

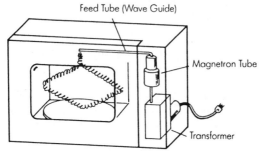

Feed Tube (Wave Guide)

Magnetron Tube

Transformer

The power cord conducts electricity to a transformer. The transformer converts low-voltage electricity into high-voltage electricity to empower the magnetron tube. The magnetron tube produces microwave energy and directs it down a feed tube into the microwave oven. The microwaves bounce off the acrylic-covered metal interior of the oven.

• The microwaves are reflected by metal.

• The microwaves pass through glass, paper, and plastic products.

• The microwaves are attracted to water, fat, and sugar.

IS STANDING TIME IMPORTANT?

Standing time is one of the most important principles in microwaving cooking. It refers to the time immediately after the microwave oven has shut off.

Standing time is the time that the food continues to cook while the vibrating molecules slow down from the very rapid microwaving vibrations of two and one-half billion times per second. The microwave oven is shut off. No microwaves are in the food. *But the food is still cooking!* (You can let the food stand in the microwave oven or on the counter if you need to use the microwave oven in the meantime.)

Standing time is part of the recipe's cooking time. Most recipes will say something like this: Microwave 10 minutes and let stand 3 minutes. The total cooking time of the food is really 13 minutes.

SHOULD I "ROTATE," OR TURN, THE DISH
WHEN MICROWAVING?

The ability of microwave ovens to cook evenly has improved greatly during the last five to ten years. Still, some microwave ovens have poor cooking patterns. Often all parts of the oven do not receive the same amount of microwaves. The food will be cooked well on one side, undercooked in the center, and overcooked on the other side.

- If you notice that food does not cook evenly in your oven, rotate the dish one-quarter turn partway through the cooking time of most recipes (or as directed) to ensure even cooking. Baked goods or foods that contain eggs (cakes, breads, custards, etc.) are most likely to need rotation.

- If your microwave has a turntable, rotating the food may not be necessary.

WHICH POWER LEVEL SHOULD I USE?

Just as you would not cook all of your foods in a conventional oven at 500°F., so, too, you should not microwave all foods at HIGH (100%).

The various (and lower) power levels cycle the microwave energy on and off to allow for slower and more even cooking. This allows time for the heat to spread to the cooler and uncooked areas.

Although many microwave oven manufacturers have tried to standardize the names of the different power levels, varying power level names abound. Some microwave ovens even use percentages instead of names for the power levels. The following chart lists the various names used for the different power levels and the percentage of microwave energy associated with each power level.

VARIABLE POWER LEVELS CHART

NAME OF POWER LEVEL	% OF POWER	FOODS THAT COOK BEST AT THIS POWER LEVEL
HIGH or FULL POWER	100%	Small amount of food that cooks quickly; candies, beverages, and vegetables.
MEDIUM HIGH or ROAST	70%	All foods that are to be reheated; eggs, appetizers, and soups.
MEDIUM or SIMMER or BAKE	50%	Stews, some cakes, yeast breads, and quiches.
DEFROST or MEDIUM LOW	30%	All foods that are to be defrosted, cakes, quick breads, cheesecakes, and tough meats.
LOW or WARM	10%	Butter and cream cheese and all foods that need to be softened or kept warm.

WHAT CAN I DO IF MY MICROWAVE OVEN HAS ONLY ONE POWER LEVEL?

You can reduce the power level/setting HIGH (100%) to MEDIUM HIGH (70%) by placing a custard cup filled with 1 cup of water in the back of your microwave oven. The water will attract some of the microwaves and lower the power level. While this method does not always work perfectly, many people have found this technique helpful.

In compact ovens (500 watts), you can successfully substitute HIGH (100%) power for MEDIUM HIGH (70%) power because the wattages are equivalent. MEDIUM HIGH (70%) in a full-size microwave oven (600/700 watts) equals HIGH (100%) in a compact oven.

ARE THERE ANY SPECIFIC ADJUSTMENTS TO MAKE WHEN USING A COMPACT MICROWAVE OVEN (450 TO 500 WATTS) IN THESE RECIPES?

Some of the recipes have compact microwave oven variations and instructions. Here are a few additional tips to keep in mind:

• Cooking at HIGH (100%) power in a 500-watt oven is similar to cooking at MEDIUM HIGH (70%) in a 700-watt oven.

• Therefore, COMPACT OVEN OWNERS SHOULD USE ONE POWER LEVEL HIGHER THAN MOST (600 to 700-watt) RECIPES INDICATE. (For example, if a recipe recommends cooking at DEFROST (30%), use MEDIUM (50%); if it recommends MEDIUM (50%), use MEDIUM HIGH (70%); if it recommends MEDIUM HIGH (70%), use HIGH (100%).

• If a recipe recommends cooking at HIGH (100%), add at least ⅛ to ¼ more time than is recommended.

SHOULD I USE THE SHORTEST OR THE LONGEST AMOUNT OF TIME LISTED IN A MICROWAVE RECIPE?

As microwave ovens can be purchased in different sizes with varying wattages, a range of cooking times is listed for each microwave recipe. This cookbook is especially designed for use with 600- to 700-watt ovens.

• 700-watt ovens cook the fastest. Use the shortest amount of time.

• 650/600-watt ovens cook quickly but not as fast as the 700-watt ovens. Use a time in the middle of the range of cooking times listed.

• 400/500-watt ovens are compact microwave ovens and, therefore, cook slower. Use the longest cooking time listed. (Compact ovens often need one-eighth to one-quarter more time than a general microwave recipe recommends.)

WHEN SHOULD FOODS BE COVERED IN THE MICROWAVE?

Food should be covered when the recipe recommends it or when moisture or steam should be retained in cooking, as in vegetables or casseroles.

- **Cover tightly** means to use a matching lid or plastic wrap.

- **Cover with vented plastic wrap** means to cover tightly with plastic wrap but leave a small edge turned back on the plastic wrap for a vent so the plastic doesn't split and so a burst of steam does not burn your hand.

- **Cover loosely** means to use waxed paper, a paper towel, or a paper napkin so that steam can escape to prevent sogginess, as in breads and meats.

- **Microwave uncovered** means the food needs drying rather than moisture, heats quickly, and usually will not spatter.

WHAT IS SHIELDING?

Shielding means to cover corners of square or rectangular baking dishes and bony pieces and edges of foods with aluminum foil. This will prevent these areas from overcooking during microwaving.

- Use only small pieces of foil.

- Never cover more than one-quarter of the food you are microwaving with foil.

CAN ALUMINUM FOIL BE USED IN ANY MICROWAVE OVEN?

Most microwave ovens manufactured since 1980 were built with specially protected magnetron tubes that allow for the use of small amounts of metal without damage to the tube.

- Read the instruction book that comes with your microwave oven to determine if you can use foil in your oven. Check under "poultry" for details, as manufacturers often recommend shielding turkey wings and legs during microwaving.

WARNING: DO NOT USE FOIL UNLESS YOUR MANUFACTURER'S INSTRUCTION BOOK RECOMMENDS IT!

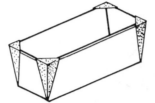

Shielding Tips

For rectangular or square dishes:

- Cut four squares or triangles of aluminum foil to cover corners of food and pan to prevent overcooking and hardening. Remove foil the last 2 to 3 minutes of microwaving time for cakes, breads, and bars.

For small or bony pieces of meat or poultry:

- Wrap aluminum foil around those pieces to prevent them from overcooking and drying out. Most meat and poultry pieces need shielding during only half the cooking time.

HOW DO I USE A TEMPERATURE PROBE?

A temperature probe is the heat-sensing accessory that comes with many microwave ovens. When the probe is attached to the microwave oven and programmed, the oven will automatically shut off when the internal temperature of the food reaches the temperature you programmed.

To work accurately, the probe must be inserted two-thirds

of the way into the center of the food. Do not allow it to touch the bone or fatty layer of the food.

After inserting the probe into the food, program both the temperature and the power level on your microwave oven. (Many recipes in this cookbook list temperatures so you can use your probe.) During standing time your food will usually rise 10 to 15 degrees more, so temperatures to which you set the probe will be lower than those required with a conventional thermometer.

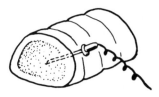

DO I NEED TO USE A TEMPERATURE PROBE?

Many recipes in this cookbook sometimes list both cooking time and temperature so you can use your probe if you like. However, it is not necessary. Using a probe can be helpful when microwaving meat or poultry or when internal temperature accuracy is important to avoid overcooking the food.

The probe will not work for microwaving candy syrups because it programs only to 200°F.

WHAT IS COMBINATION COOKING?

Combination cooking refers to the use of both your range and microwave oven in a recipe. It can cut the cooking time for some foods by up to 50 percent. In combination cooking, many recipes are started in the conventional range to ensure browning and then transferred to the microwave oven to speed cooking.

WHAT IS A CONVECTION MICROWAVE OVEN?

A convection microwave is a convection oven and a microwave oven. Convection cooking is simply "fan-forced hot air." In a convection oven, a high-speed fan circulates hot air throughout the oven cavity. The moving air surrounds the food and quickly seals in the juices.

In convection microwaving, the microwaves cycle on and off with this fan-forced hot air, producing traditionally browned and crisped foods in half the time of a regular/conventional oven.

Some convection microwave recipes are included in this cookbook. Adaptations for combination cooking, combining your regular oven with your microwave oven to produce similar results, are also given for those who do not have a convection microwave.

WHICH CONVECTION MICROWAVE OVEN SETTING SHOULD I USE?

Convection microwave ovens use different terms for oven settings. Each convection microwave recipe in this book gives possible names of settings on your microwave oven. Choose the setting that matches the wording on your oven. (For example, Low-Mix Bake 350°F on one oven is about the same as Code #2 on another oven or Combination 2 on still another oven.)

ANSWERS TO YOUR QUESTIONS ABOUT HOLIDAY MICROWAVING

Can I convert my conventional holiday recipes to micro-wave recipes?

YES! YES! YES! Converting conventional recipes to microwave recipes can easily be done with the help of the following tips:

MICROWAVE ADAPTATION TIPS FOR
CONVENTIONAL HOLIDAY RECIPES

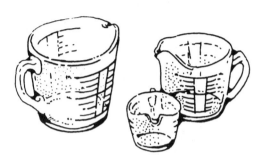

- **Reduce time** for conventional cooking by approximately 50 to 75 percent.

- **Reduce leavening ingredients** (baking powder, baking soda, etc.) by one-half to avoid an overleavened taste and to prevent cakes and breads from over-rising.

- **Reduce liquid ingredients** by 1 tablespoon per cup because very little liquid evaporates during cooking in a microwave oven.

- **Use a microwave candy thermometer** for easiest adaptation of candy recipes. (Many candy recipes do not need any special adjustment in ingredients.)

- **Use a large 2- to 3-quart microwave-safe bowl** for candy recipes as ingredients will "boil up" more than on the rangetop. Do not try to double microwave candy recipes. Boilovers are messy.

- **Always prepare a microwave-safe cake pan, loaf pan, or tube pan** by greasing with oil (or spraying with shortening) and then dusting with sugar. (If you dust with flour the cake will stick to the pan.)

- **Place cake, pie, or bread dishes** on an inverted saucer or pie plate while microwaving to ensure that the microwaves bounce off the bottom of the oven and penetrate the bottom of the food and it gets done.

- **Follow a similar recipe** in a microwave cookbook, substituting your own ingredients.

- **Shield corners of square or rectangular dishes with foil** to prevent hardened corners when microwave-baking. (See page 9, Shielding Tips.)

- **Read the Answers to Basic Microwave Questions** (pages 3–11) as a helpful reference for general microwave cooking questions.

WHAT BASIC MICROWAVE COOKWARE DO I NEED?

The following list of basic cookware is especially recommended for holiday microwave baking and dessert-making.

Basic Microwave Cookware (in glass or microwave-safe plastic)

Keep in mind that most of your glass cookware, such as Pyrex®, Corningware®, and Fire King ®, will work well in the microwave oven (Corelle® *cannot* be used).

- Custard cups: 6- and 10-ounce sets

- Bowls and/or measuring cups: 1- and 2-cup; 1- and 2-quart

- Bundt or ring pan: 8- and 12-cup

- Pie plates: 8-, 9-, or 10-inch

- Cake dishes: 8- or 9-inch square/round; 8 × 12-inch rectangular

- Loaf pans: 8 × 4-inch or 9 × 5-inch

- Casseroles: 1-, 2-, and 3-quart

- Muffin pan: 6-cup

- Roasting rack: a size that fits into your microwave oven

The following basic accessories are also helpful for holiday microwave baking and dessert-making.

Optional Microwave Accessories

- Microwave candy thermometer: designed for use in the microwave.

- Microwave heat-resistant stirring spoons: that can be left in food while microwaving.

- Microwave popcorn popper: cooks popcorn safely in 3 minutes with or without oil.

In addition, you may need these disposable items:

- Paper towels (use white if possible), napkins, waxed paper, Styrofoam plates and cups, toothpicks, and plastic wrap.

WARNING:

- Do not use fine china, lead crystal, or glass trimmed with metal.

- Do not use wooden utensils because often they will crack after microwaving.

- Do not use metal except as specified for a convection microwave oven or in small amounts to shield corners of food as many microwave manufacturers now allow. Check the instruction manual that came with your oven.

HOW CAN I KNOW IF A PIECE OF COOKWARE IS MICROWAVE-SAFE?

The following test will determine if a pan, plate, dish, and so on, is microwave-proof.

```
┌─────────────────────────────────────────────┐
│                                             │
│        MICROWAVE COOKWARE TEST              │
│                                             │
│    Fill a custard cup or glass measuring    │
│  cup with 1 cup of warm water. Place the    │
│  cookware in question next to the cup of    │
│  water. (Do not allow the two to touch.)    │
│  Microwave for 1 to 1½ minutes at HIGH      │
│  (100%). The water should become very hot.  │
│  If the adjacent dish is safe for           │
│  microwaving, it will remain cool. If the   │
│  dish becomes warm, do not use it in your   │
│  microwave; it is absorbing the microwaves  │
│  and probably contains metal or metallic    │
│  paint.                                     │
│                                             │
└─────────────────────────────────────────────┘
```

WHAT SHAPES OF DISHES WORK BEST FOR MICROWAVING?

Ring-shape or round dishes work best for microwaving because the microwaves can penetrate the food evenly from all sides.

Ring-shape pans and foods allow the microwaves to reach the center of foods. Therefore, the center of the food cooks as quickly as the sides and bottom cook.

A WORD ON CANDY THERMOMETERS

- For many candy recipes a microwave candy thermometer is a tremendous help. Some candy recipes require only the heating and melting of ingredients, so microwaving by time is all that is needed. Other candy recipes, involving a sugar syrup, produce the best results when a candy thermometer is used for accurate temperature-timing.

- Most candy recipes list an approximate microwaving time as a guide in addition to the finished temperature. Near the end of the recommended cooking time, carefully watch the thermometer just as you would for rangetop cooking. When the appropriate temperature is reached, immediately turn off the microwave oven.

WHAT TYPE OF CANDY THERMOMETER CAN I USE IN THE MICROWAVE?

- The easiest and most accurate results are produced with a microwave candy thermometer. It can be left in the microwave oven while cooking and often has a paddle base that can be used for stirring.

- A conventional candy thermometer will not work and is likely to shatter or break if used while microwaving. A "quick-read" candy thermometer can be inserted to give an approximate temperature immediately after the microwave oven is stopped.

- Most temperature probes that come with a microwave oven will not work with candy syrups because they register temperatures only to 200°F. A microwave candy thermometer will register temperatures from 100°F to 320°F.

WHAT IF I DON'T HAVE A MICROWAVE THERMOMETER?

Although a microwave candy thermometer produces the most accurate results and takes the guesswork out of candy making, you can still make candy successfully in the microwave oven without one.

The following standard cold-water test lists the approximate temperatures of cooked candy syrups.

OLD-FASHIONED COLD WATER TEST
for candy doneness

Drop a small amount of cooked mixture into a small cup of very cold water. Then form into a ball, if possible, and remove from the water.

Soft Ball (234°–240°F.)
A soft ball will form and flatten when removed from the water.

Firm Ball (244°–248°F.)

A firm ball will form and will not flatten but remain rounded when removed from the water.

Hard Ball (250°–266°F.)

A hard ball will form and will be very firm yet pliable when removed from the water.

Soft Crack (270°–290°F.)

Mixture will separate into threads that are hard but not brittle.

Hard Crack (300°–310°F.)

Mixture will separate into threads that are hard and brittle.

CAN SUGAR CRYSTALS BE PREVENTED IN CANDY?

Grainy or "sugary" texture in candy can be avoided. Try these hints to prevent the formation of sugar crystals.

1. *Use a clean spoon each time you stir* a candy syrup while it is cooking. (Toffees, divinities, and old-fashioned fudges are especially prone to forming large sugar crystals.)
2. If a recipe calls for butter or margarine, grease the sides of the bowl before adding any of the ingredients.
3. Use butter instead of margarine.
4. Using a damp paper towel, wipe down the sides of your bowl (to remove sugar crystals) shortly after a candy mixture has started to boil. Continue microwaving.

ARE THERE ADJUSTMENTS FOR HIGH-ALTITUDE MICROWAVING?

Microwave cooking works well at high altitudes. Less adjustment is needed to adapt microwave recipes to high altitudes than conventional recipes. This is due to the fact that microwave recipes are usually moister, less apt to dry out, and are more stable than conventional recipes.

Microwave recipes also require less leavening and larger dishes, all of which are adjustment needs for conventional high-altitude baking.

Therefore, little adjustment is needed in microwave recipes at elevations below 3,500 to 4,000 feet. At higher elevations (4,000 to 10,000 feet above sea level) some slight adjustments are recommended for a successful microwaved product due to the decreased air pressure and, therefore, lower boiling temperature of water. These recommendations are listed below.

It is always a good idea, if you are new to a high-altitude area, to check with your State or County Extension Office or consumer services department of your local utility company for specific recipe adaptation instructions for your area.

GUIDELINES FOR HIGH-ALTITUDE*
MICROWAVING

1. Use the longest microwaving time recommended for most recipes due to the lower boiling point of water at high altitudes. (Some recipes, especially vegetables and meats, will require 1 to 2 minutes additional cooking time.)
2. Increase the dish size for microwave recipes. Lower air pressure at high altitudes causes food to rise more.
3. For candy, reduce the recommended temperature cited in microwave recipes by the number of degrees difference between 212° and the lowered boiling point in your high altitude area. (For example, if the boiling point of water in your area is 204°, the difference from 212° is 8°. A candy recipe that is microwaved at sea level to 238° will be done for you at 230°.)
4. For breads or cakes, add 1 to 2 tablespoons liquid and 1 tablespoon flour to microwave recipes to increase

. . . .
*Elevations 4,000 to 10,000 feet above sea level.

moistness, improve texture, and prevent dryness caused by lowered air pressure.

5. For breads, cakes, and casseroles, always use extra-large or large eggs instead of medium, to add moistness and stability.

6. Check with your State or County Extension Office or utility company for specific adjustments for your location.

NOTES ON CHOCOLATE

——— · ❄ · ———

CAN CHOCOLATE BE MELTED
SUCCESSFULLY IN THE MICROWAVE OVEN?

Short-Cut News

The microwave oven brings "short-cut" news to those who like to work with melted chocolate. The time savings are marvelous. Scorching from direct burner heat is no longer a problem and the double boiler is no longer a necessity. The microwave oven is perfect for melting any kind of chocolate.

A Word of Caution on Melting Chocolate

If chocolate is overmicrowaved, it will become stiff and grainy. Although it will still be tasty and certainly edible, the texture and appearance cannot be repaired. Chocolate should never be covered when microwaving, as the moisture formed on the inside can also cause the chocolate to stiffen.

Melt Chocolate at 70% Power*

Although chocolate can be melted on HIGH (100%) power in the microwave oven, melt chocolate using only ME-DIUM HIGH (70%) power whenever possible to avoid over-cooking the chocolate (and the grainy/stiff appearance). Twelve ounces of chocolate chips, squares, or cubes usually require only 3 to 3½ minutes, uncovered, at MEDIUM HIGH (70%) to melt. After stirring, if more microwaving time is necessary, add only 30 seconds at a time and stir.

Melted Chocolate Turns Shiny

When microwaving chocolate chips or squares, the chocolate will look soft, puffy, and shiny but will not appear melted. It will become smooth and look melted after stirring. The hint that the chocolate has melted will be its change from a dull chocolate color to a shiny chocolate surface.

WHAT TYPE OF CHOCOLATE COATING SHOULD I USE FOR MICROWAVE CANDY MAKING?

Chocolate almond bark produces the best coating for candy because it does not soften at room temperature. To produce similar results with chocolate chips, add ¼ cup finely grated food-grade (edible) paraffin wax to the chips before microwaving.

Paraffin wax cannot be heated alone in a microwave oven. However, when added to the chocolate, the heat from the chocolate will melt the wax. Candy dipped in the chocolate-paraffin mixture will remain firm at room temperature.

. . . .
*If you have a compact microwave oven (400 to 500 watts), melt chocolate at HIGH (100%) power.

EASY CHOCOLATE CANDY COATING

2 cups semisweet chocolate chips
¼ cup grated food-grade paraffin wax

Microwave for 3 minutes at MEDIUM HIGH (70%).
Stir until smooth. Microwave again for 1 to 1½ minutes at
MEDIUM HIGH (70%), if necessary. Stir until smooth.

White chocolate can be substituted for the chocolate chips, but microwave at MEDIUM (50%) instead of MEDIUM HIGH (70%).

ANY SUGGESTIONS FOR EASY CLEANUP?

You can clean your sticky and syrup-baked-on microwave bowls easily using the microwave. Simply add 1 cup water to the bowl. Cover with a paper towel or waxed paper. Microwave for 4 to 5 minutes at HIGH (100%).

Presto! The steam and water will clean the bottom and sides of the bowl.

SWEETENED CONDENSED MILK SUBSTITUTE

· · · · ·

An easy substitute for one 14-ounce-can sweetened condensed milk

½ cup water   ¾ cup sugar
1½ cups nonfat dry milk   1½ teaspoons vanilla

Combine water and dry milk in a 1-quart microwave-safe bowl; stir in sugar and vanilla. Microwave for 1½ to 2 minutes at MEDIUM HIGH (70%) until very hot, stirring twice. (Do not boil.)

SUBSTITUTIONS—IN A PINCH

The following foods can be substituted for those listed.

FOR	YOU CAN USE
1 ounce baking chocolate square	3 tablespoons cocoa plus 1 tablespoon shortening/margarine
6 ounces (1 cup) semisweet chocolate chips	1/3 cup cocoa plus 1/3 cup sugar plus 1/4 cup shortening
4-ounce bar sweet (German) chocolate	1/4 cup cocoa plus 1/4 cup sugar plus 2 tablespoons shortening
1 tablespoon cornstarch	2 tablespoons flour (or) 1 1/2 tablespoons tapioca
1 cup milk	1/2 cup evaporated milk plus 1/2 cup water
1 cup buttermilk	1 tablespoon lemon juice or vinegar plus enough milk to make 1 cup
1 cup half-and-half	7/8 cup milk plus 3 tablespoons butter
1 cup heavy cream	3/4 cup milk plus 1/3 cup butter
1 cup whipping cream, whipped	2 cups whipped topping
1 teaspoon baking powder	1/4 teaspoon baking soda and 1 teaspoon cream of tartar
1 cup miniature marshmallows	11 large marshmallows, cut up
1 cup brown sugar	1 cup white sugar mixed with 1 tablespoon dark molasses
1 cup corn syrup	1 cup sugar plus 1/4 cup liquid
1 whole egg medium/large	2 egg yolks
3 tablespoons fresh herbs	1 tablespoon dried herbs
1 clove garlic	1/8 teaspoon garlic powder

COMMON FOOD EQUIVALENTS

FOR	YOU CAN USE
1/4 pound butter or margarine	1 stick or 1/2 cup
1 cup shredded cheese	4 ounces
1 cup cottage cheese	8 ounces
1 cup chocolate chips	6 ounces
1 1/3 cups coconut	4 ounces
1 cup whipping cream	2 cups whipped
1 pound flour	3 1/2 cups
1 pound brown sugar, packed	2 1/4 cups
1 pound powdered (confectioner's) sugar	3 3/4 cups
1 pound granulated sugar	2 1/4 cups
1 medium lemon	2 1/2 tablespoons lemon juice + 2 teaspoons peel
1 medium orange	1/3 cup juice + 1 tablespoon peel
1 pound banana (3–4 medium)	2 cups mashed
1 pound apples (3 large)	3 cups pared and sliced
1 cup bread crumbs	2–3 slices bread
1 pound dates	2 cups chopped
1 quart strawberries	4 cups sliced
1 medium peach/pear	1/2 cup sliced
1 pound walnuts or pecans	3 3/4 to 4 cups chopped
1 pound raisins	2 3/4 cups

HOLIDAY APPETIZERS

· ❄ ·

STUFFED MUSHROOMS

· · · · ·

1–1½ pounds fresh
mushrooms (about 24,
1½ inches each)
¼ pound bulk sausage

¼ cup chopped green
onion (optional)
8 ounces cream cheese,
softened*
2–4 drops Tabasco sauce

1. Clean mushrooms. Remove and chop stems. Place 12
mushrooms on a glass pie plate. Microwave for 1 to 1½
minutes at HIGH (100%). Drain and set aside. Repeat.
2. Microwave sausage, chopped mushroom stems, and onion
(if desired), in a small microwave-safe casserole covered
with a paper towel or waxed paper, for 3 to 4 minutes at
HIGH (100%) until sausage is no longer pink. Drain
well.

*Soften cream cheese by leaving it at room temperature for 30 minutes *or* by
microwaving it, unwrapped, for 1 to 1½ minutes at MEDIUM HIGH (70%).

TIPS

When selecting mush-
rooms, choose those
that are without blem-
ish, light in color, and
about the same size.

To prepare them: Rinse
quickly in a colander
under cold water and
pat dry.

The mushroom caps can
be prepared ahead of
time and refrigerated
until needed. After mi-
crowaving the caps in
step #1, wrap in plastic
wrap and refrigerate.

Prepare the filling following steps #2 and #3; cover with plastic wrap and refrigerate.

Bring mushrooms and filling to room temperature about ½ hour before preparing and serving in step #4.

T I P S
· · · · · · · ·

If you are fond of Reuben sandwiches, you will love this appetizer!

Be sure to use the traditional "thick" Thousand Island dressing.

3. Stir softened cream cheese into sausage. Add Tabasco. Set aside until just before serving time.
4. Stuff mushroom caps by placing 1 tablespoon of prepared mixture in each cap. On a serving plate, microwave, 12 at a time, for 2 to 2½ minutes at MEDIUM HIGH (70%), until hot. Serve immediately.

Yield: Approximately 24 appetizers.

———————— · ❄ · ————————

MINI REUBENS
———————— · · · · · ————————

Tasty appetizers for any holiday.

½ cup Swiss cheese, grated (2 ounces)
½ cup sauerkraut, drained and cut up
2 tablespoons Thousand Island dressing

1 cup cooked corned beef, chopped finely
40–50 melba rye toast rounds (approximately 5½ ounce box)

1. Combine all the ingredients except the melba toast. Cover and refrigerate until ready to serve or proceed with step #2, and serve immediately.
2. Five minutes before serving, place heaping teaspoonfuls on melba toast. Microwave, 10 at a time, on a microwave-safe plate for 40 to 50 seconds at MEDIUM HIGH (70%). Repeat. Delicious!

Yield: 40 to 50 appetizers.

———————— · ❄ · ————————

· ·

Making marriage work is like running a farm. You have to start all over again each morning.

GLAZED MIXED NUTS

· · · · ·

2 large egg whites
1 cup sugar

16–24-ounce package
   mixed nuts
2 tablespoons butter or
   margarine

1. Beat egg whites in a bowl until stiff. Stir in sugar. Add nuts. Set aside.
2. Microwave butter in a 8 × 12-inch microwave-safe dish (or 10-inch pie plate) for 25 to 30 seconds at HIGH (100%). Add coated nuts.
3. Microwave for 9 to 10 minutes at HIGH (100%), until glazed, stirring twice. Spread on waxed paper to cool. Break apart. Store loosely covered, *not* in an airtight container.

Yield: 30 to 40 servings.

———— · ❄ · ————

CHEESE AND OLIVE SPREAD ON BAGLETS

(OR ENGLISH MUFFINS OR CRACKERS)

· · · · ·

4 slices bacon
1 cup grated cheese (4 ounces) (Swiss or Cheddar)
2 tablespoons black olives
2 tablespoons onion, chopped fine
½ cup mayonnaise

2 tablespoons chopped nuts
12 baglets (miniature bagels), or 16 crackers, or 6 English muffins

1. Microwave bacon on a paper towel–lined plate, covered with a paper towel, for 3 to 4 minutes at HIGH (100%). Crumble.

. . . .

Recipe for making up after a quarrel: It takes two.

A mixture of pecans, almonds, cashews, walnuts, and dry-roasted peanuts works especially well.

If you use crackers, buy sturdy, crisp ones so they don't become soggy after microwaving.

Microwave crackers on two layers of paper toweling so the moisture is absorbed and crackers do not become soggy.

Baglets are miniature bagels. They can be found in the freezer-bread section of your grocery store.

2. Combine crumbled bacon and remaining ingredients (except baglets) in a bowl. Split baglets.

3. Spread mixture on baglets (or split and toasted English muffins, or crackers). Microwave 12 split baglets (or 6 split English muffins, or 8 crackers) for 2 to 2½ minutes at MEDIUM HIGH (70%), until cheese is bubbly. Repeat with remaining baglets. Serve immediately.

Yield: 24 baglets.

———————— · ❄ · ————————

DIPS

. ❄ .

HOT CRAB DIP

8-ounce package cream
   cheese

3 tablespoons mayonnaise

2 tablespoons white wine

1 teaspoon prepared
   mustard (Dijon)

½ teaspoon sugar (or sugar
   substitute)

Dash of seasoned salt

7½-ounce can crab meat

Slivered almonds and
   chopped parsley to
   garnish (optional)

1. Microwave cream cheese, unwrapped, for 1 to 1½ minutes at MEDIUM HIGH (70%) in a 1-quart microwave-
   safe bowl until soft. Stir in remaining ingredients.
2. Microwave for 4 to 5 minutes at MEDIUM HIGH (70%)
   (or to 130°F. if using a probe). Serve warm garnished
   with slivered almonds and chopped parsley, along with a
   plate of crackers and/or fresh vegetables.

Yield: 8 to 12 servings.

. ❄ .

TIPS

To lower the calories in
this delicious dip with-
out losing the flavor:
Substitute Neufchatel
cheese for the cream
cheese, reduced-calo-
rie mayonnaise for the
mayonnaise, and apple
juice for the white
wine.

This warmed dip is the perfect appetizer to serve on cold winter evenings.

CHIPPED BEEF DIP ON MELBA ROUNDS

——————— · · · · · ———————

8-ounce package cream cheese	¼ teaspoon garlic powder
8-ounce carton sour cream	3 ounces chipped beef, chopped
½ onion (¼ cup) diced fine	1 package melba toast rounds, any flavor

1. Place cream cheese in a 1-quart microwave-safe casserole. Microwave, unwrapped, for 1 to 1½ minutes at MEDIUM HIGH (70%), until soft. Add remaining ingredients, except melba toast. Blend well.
2. Microwave for 6 minutes at MEDIUM HIGH (70%),* stirring once, until very warm.
3. Serve on melba toast rounds. (Heat plate of rounds, spread with dip, for 1 minute at MEDIUM HIGH (70%) before serving, if desired.) Or serve dip in a chafing dish with assorted crackers nearby.

Yield: 8 to 12 servings.

——————— · ❄ · ———————

CREAMY FRUIT DIP

——————— · · · · · ———————

A delightful accompaniment to a fruit tray!

Serve this refreshing dip with stemmed fresh strawberries, sliced kiwi and nectarines, grapes, and cherries.

8-ounce package cream cheese	1 teaspoon vanilla
½ cup powdered sugar	8 ounces whipped topping (3½ cups)
4 tablespoons frozen orange juice concentrate	

···

*Compacts: Microwave at HIGH (100%) for 5 to 6 minutes.

1. Microwave unwrapped cream cheese in a 2-quart micro-wave-safe bowl for 1 to 1½ minutes at MEDIUM HIGH (70%). Beat in powdered sugar, orange juice concentrate, and vanilla.
2. Fold in the whipped topping. Chill at least one hour. Serve with a tray of fresh fruit.

Yield: 12 to 20 servings.

——————— · ❄ · ———————

Middle age is when you know all the answers and nobody ever asks you the questions.

HOLIDAY BAR
COOKIES

· ❄ ·

TIPS

If you need a fast but delicious dessert, this is the one!

To avoid having to shield the corners with foil, use a round 8-inch microwave-safe casserole dish or cake pan. (Since there are no corners to overcook on a round pan, you won't need to use foil strips.)

JIFFY BLACK FOREST CAKE BARS

· · · · ·

You won't believe how tasty these are!

21-ounce can cherry pie
   filling
1½ cups dry chocolate
   cake mix, or 9-ounce
   package Jiffy chocolate
   cake mix

3 tablespoons butter or
   margarine, sliced
½ cup brown sugar,
   packed
½ cup chopped nuts or
   sliced almonds
   (optional)

1. Grease and sugar an 8 × 8-inch microwave-safe pan. Layer all ingredients in the order given.
2. Shield the corners of the pan with foil strips (optional).

3. Microwave for 10 to 11 minutes at HIGH (100%).,* †
   (Remove foil strips the last 5 minutes.)
4. Let stand until cooled to set.

Yield: 16 to 24 bars.

——————— · ❄ · ———————

S'MORE BARS

——————— · · · · · ———————

A fun treat for the kids to make and enjoy!

⅓ cup light corn syrup
1 cup (6 ounces) semisweet
   chocolate chips
½ teaspoon vanilla

2 cups miniature
   marshmallows
4 cups honey graham
   cereal (Golden Grahams)

1. Microwave corn syrup in a 2-quart microwave-safe bowl
   for 1 minute at HIGH (100%), or until boiling. Stir in
   chocolate chips. Microwave 20 to 30 seconds at HIGH
   (100%). Stir until smooth. Add vanilla.
2. Stir in marshmallows until well coated. Fold in cereal.
   Pour into a buttered 9 × 13-inch pan. Spread and press
   into bars with a buttered spoon. Cool. Cut into bars.

Yield: 36 bars.

——————— · ❄ · ———————

*Rotate dish once, if necessary, for even cooking.
....
†Compacts: Microwave for 12 minutes at HIGH (100%) in step #3.

....
*Lots of things can be accomplished in a day—if you don't make that
day tomorrow.*

S'more Bars are a variation of my favorite treat made as a child at Girl Scout camp. We would toast marshmallows over a campfire until they were golden brown, then sandwich them with a chocolate bar between two graham crackers. We would eat them and exclaim "some more, please."

To make a S'more in the microwave oven: Place ½ square chocolate bar (like Hershey's) on a graham cracker square; top with a marshmallow; microwave for 15 to 20 seconds at HIGH (100%) until marshmallow puffs. Place another cracker on top. Let stand 30 seconds. Enjoy!

You can use a metal
baking dish, if you like,
because it will not be
used in the microwave
oven.

Garnish these delicious
bars with additional
chopped pecans or use
a pecan half on each
bar.

GERMAN CHOCOLATE PECAN BARS

·········· — · · · · · — ··········

························· BARS ·····················

6 graham crackers
1 cup brown sugar,
  packed
1 stick (½ cup) butter or
  margarine, softened
2 large eggs, beaten

½ cup milk
½ cup quick oatmeal
  (uncooked)
1 cup shredded coconut
1 cup chopped pecans
  (4 ounces)
1 teaspoon vanilla

························· FROSTING ·····················

½ stick (¼ cup) butter or
  margarine
3 tablespoons
  unsweetened cocoa

3 tablespoons milk
2 cups powdered sugar
1 teaspoon vanilla

1. **Bars:** Line the bottom of an 8 × 12-inch or 9 × 13-inch baking dish with the graham crackers. (Cut graham crackers to fit.)
2. Combine brown sugar, butter, eggs, and milk in a 2-quart microwave-safe bowl.
3. Microwave for 3 to 4 minutes at HIGH (100%). Stir in oatmeal. Microwave again for 4 to 5 minutes at MEDIUM HIGH (70%) until very thick, stirring twice.
4. Stir in coconut, pecans, and vanilla. Spread over crackers. Let stand 10 minutes.
5. **Frosting:** Microwave butter for 30 to 40 seconds at HIGH (100%) in a 1-quart microwave-safe bowl. Stir in cocoa. Blend in milk. Beat in powdered sugar and vanilla until smooth. Frost bars.

Yield: 24 bars.

——— · ❄ · ———

CHOCOLATE SYRUP BROWNIES

————— · · · · · —————

A famous recipe adapted for the microwave

···················· BROWNIES ·····················

1½ sticks (¾ cup) butter
  or margarine
1 cup sugar
4 medium eggs, beaten
1 teaspoon vanilla

16-ounce can chocolate
  syrup
1 cup flour
¼ teaspoon baking
  powder

················· FROSTING (OPTIONAL) ·················

2 tablespoons butter or
  margarine
1 cup sugar
¼ cup milk

½ cup milk chocolate
  chips (3 ounces)
1 teaspoon vanilla

················· TOPPING (OPTIONAL) ·················

½ cup (2 ounces) chopped
  walnuts or peanuts

1. **Brownies:** Microwave butter in a mixing bowl for 20 to
   30 seconds at HIGH (100%) to soften. Beat in sugar,
   eggs, and vanilla until creamy. Stir in chocolate syrup;
   mix in flour and baking powder.
2. Pour into an 8 × 12-inch microwave-safe baking dish that
   has been greased and sugared. Shield corners with foil.
   Microwave for 8 minutes at HIGH (100%).* Remove
   shielding. Microwave again for 3 to 4½ minutes at

··

*Rotate dish twice, if necessary, for even cooking.

··

*Let others share your sunny days, and you will find it true that others
will be glad to share the rainy days with you.*

TIPS
········

This is the traditional brownie recipe made with chocolate syrup. Use Hershey's for best results.

Do *not* grease and flour the pan (the grease and flour would bake in a separate layer). Grease and *sugar* the pan instead.

You can also make this recipe in an 8-inch square baking dish. The time and power levels are approximately the same; shield the corners. (See page 9 for tips on shielding corners.)

HIGH (100%). Let stand 5 minutes. Sprinkle with powdered sugar or frost.

3. **Frosting:** In a 1-quart microwave-safe bowl, combine
butter, sugar, and milk. Microwave for 2 to 3 minutes at
HIGH (100%), until mixture boils. Stir in chocolate
chips and vanilla until smooth. Frost brownies immediately. Sprinkle with nuts for a topping, if desired.

Yield: 24 bars.

————— · ❄ · —————

PEANUT BUTTER FUDGE BROWNIES

————— · · · · · —————

For peanut butter lovers everywhere!

············· BROWNIES ·············

⅓ cup butter or margarine
⅓ cup unsweetened cocoa
1 cup sugar
2 medium eggs
1 teaspoon vanilla

½ teaspoon baking
  powder
¾ cup flour
¼ cup peanut butter

············· FROSTING (OPTIONAL) ·············

2 tablespoons creamy
  peanut butter
1 tablespoon butter or
  margarine
¾ cup sugar

3 tablespoons milk
½ cup (3 ounces)
  semisweet chocolate
  chips

············· TOPPING (OPTIONAL) ·············

½ cup (2 ounces) chopped
  peanuts

TIPS

········

For easy Fudge
Brownies: Follow the
same recipe, omitting
the peanut butter and
increasing the butter
from ⅓ cup to ½ cup.

For Chocolate Fudge
Frosting: Omit the pea-
nut butter and increase
the butter from 1 table-
spoon to 2 table-
spoons.

(See page 9 for tips on
shielding corners.)

1. **Brownies:** Microwave butter and cocoa in a 2-quart microwave-safe bowl for 1 minute at HIGH (100%). Stir in sugar thoroughly.
2. Blend in eggs and vanilla.
3. Combine baking powder and flour and add to cocoa batter. Stir until well blended.
4. Spread into a greased and sugared 8-inch square microwave-safe baking dish.
5. Microwave peanut butter in a small microwave-safe bowl for 1 minute at HIGH (100%). Spoon over batter and swirl gently with a knife to produce a marbled effect. Shield corners with foil. Cover with waxed paper.
6. Microwave for 4 minutes at HIGH (100%).* Remove foil shielding. Cover. Microwave again for 1½ to 2 minutes at HIGH (100%). Let stand 5 minutes. Frost, if desired, and top with peanuts.
7. **Frosting:** Combine peanut butter, butter, sugar, and milk in a 1-quart microwave-safe bowl. Microwave for 2 minutes at HIGH (100%), or until mixture boils. Stir in chocolate chips until smooth. Frost brownies immediately. Sprinkle with peanuts for a topping, if desired.

Yield: 16 to 24 bars.

———————— · ❄ · ————————

*Rotate pan twice, if necessary, for even cooking.

Middle age is that period in life when our broad mind and narrow waist begin to exchange places.

FRUIT OR NUT BARS

❄

TIPS
....

Use a small sharp hand grater or "zester" to grate only the yellow outer layer of the lemon peel, called the zest. Avoid using any of the white pith beneath the zest because it has a bitter flavor.

(See page 9 for tips on shielding corners.)

LEMON BARS DELUXE

· · · · ·

················· CRUST ·················

1 stick (½ cup) butter or
  margarine

1 cup flour
½ cup powdered sugar

················· LEMON FILLING ·················

2 medium eggs
1 cup sugar
3 tablespoons lemon juice

½ teaspoon baking
  powder
1½ tablespoons flour
1 teaspoon grated lemon
  peel (zest only)

1. **Crust:** Microwave butter in an 8- or 9-inch square microwave-safe baking dish for 20 to 30 seconds at HIGH (100%), until soft. Combine flour and powdered sugar;

stir into butter until crumbly. Press mixture into bottom of dish to form crust. Microwave for 3½ to 4 minutes at HIGH (100%).

2. **Lemon Filling:** Beat eggs and sugar in a mixing bowl until fluffy. Stir in the lemon juice, baking powder, flour and lemon peel. Blend until smooth. Pour over the microwaved crust. Shield corners with foil.

3. Microwave for 3½ minutes at HIGH (100%). Remove foil shielding. Continue to microwave for 1 to 2 minutes at HIGH (100%), until almost set. Let stand 10 to 15 minutes. (Filling will set completely.) Sprinkle with powdered sugar and cut into bars.

Yield: 16 bars.

———— · ❄ · ————

LEMON MACAROON BARS

A delicious lemon bar with coconut!

···························· CRUST ·····························

1 stick (½ cup) butter or margarine
1 cup flour

½ cup brown sugar, packed
¼ cup flaked coconut

················ COCONUT LEMON FILLING ················

3 medium eggs, beaten
1½ cups sugar
¼ cup flour

1 teaspoon baking powder
½ cup flaked coconut
¼ cup lemon juice

A house is made of bricks and stones, but a home is made of love alone.

1. **Crust:** Microwave butter in a 8 × 12-inch microwave-safe baking dish for 20 to 30 seconds at HIGH (100%) until soft. Combine flour, brown sugar, and coconut; stir into butter until crumbly. Press mixture into bottom of dish to form crust. Microwave for 3½ to 4 minutes at HIGH (100%).

2. **Coconut Lemon Filling:** Beat eggs and sugar in a 2-quart microwave-safe bowl until fluffy. Stir in the flour, baking powder, coconut, and lemon juice. Blend until smooth. Microwave for 4 to 5½ minutes at HIGH (100%).

3. Spread filling over crust. Microwave for 1½ to 2 minutes at HIGH (100%) to set. Let stand 10 to 15 minutes. Sprinkle with powdered sugar and cut into bars. Refrigerate.

Yield: 24 bars.

· ❄ ·

MICHELLE'S BUTTER PECAN BARS

· · · · ·

················· CRUST ·················

1 cup flour	1 stick (½ cup) butter or
¼ cup powdered sugar	margarine

················· FILLING ·················

14-ounce can sweetened	1 egg beaten
condensed milk	1 teaspoon vanilla

················· TOPPING ·················

1 cup chopped pecans	1 cup almond brickle
	chips (6 ounces)

1. **Crust:** Microwave butter in an 8 × 8-inch microwave-safe baking dish for 20 to 30 seconds at HIGH (100%) until

You can substitute butterscotch chips or chocolate chips for the almond brickle chips.

Hershey's almond brickle chips work the best.

soft. Combine ingredients until crumbly using a fork, pastry blender, or food processor. Press into bottom of dish to form crust. Microwave for 3½ to 4 minutes at HIGH (100%). Set aside.

2. **Filling:** Beat ingredients until well blended in a 2-quart microwave-safe bowl. Microwave for 4 to 5 minutes at MEDIUM (50%). (Mixture will start to set.) Stir and pour over cooked crust.

3. Microwave for 9 to 10 minutes at MEDIUM (50%), until almost set. Sprinkle with topping ingredients. Microwave for 1½ to 2½ minutes at HIGH (100%) to set. Cool.

Yield: 16 bars.

———————— · ❄ · ————————

EASY HAWAIIAN BARS

———————— · · · · · ————————

8 ounces crushed
   pineapple, drained well
20-ounce can cherry pie
   filling
1½ cups dry white or
   yellow cake mix, or 9-
   ounce cake mix

⅓ cup butter or
   margarine, sliced
⅓ cup brown sugar,
   packed and crumbled

TIPS
....
If you don't shield the corners with foil, they will overcook slightly. However, in this recipe, the crunchy corners are quite tasty.

1. Grease and sugar an 8 × 8-inch microwave-safe pan. Layer all ingredients in the pan in order given.
2. Shield the corners of the pan with foil strips (optional).
3. Microwave for 10 to 11 minutes at HIGH (100%).* † (Remove foil strips the last 5 minutes.)
4. Let stand until cooled to set.

Yield: 16 bars.

———————— · ❄ · ————————

....

*Rotate dish once, if necessary, for even cooking.

†Compacts: Microwave for 12 minutes at high (100%) in Step #3.

DATE DELIGHT SQUARES

· · · · ·

························ CRUST ························

1 stick (½ cup) butter or
   margarine
½ cup brown sugar,
   packed

1 cup flour
1 teaspoon vanilla
¼ cup (1 ounce) chopped
   nuts

····················· DATE FILLING ·····················

1¼ cups (8 ounces) dates,
   chopped
¾ cup water
1 tablespoon lemon juice

2 cups miniature
   marshmallows (22 large
   marshmallows)
Whipped topping, to
   garnish (optional)

1. **Crust:** Microwave butter in a 9-inch square microwave-safe baking dish for 40 to 60 seconds on HIGH (100%), or until melted.* Stir in brown sugar, flour, vanilla, and nuts. Press mixture into bottom of pan. Microwave for 4 to 5 minutes at HIGH (100%), or until lightly browned and no longer doughy. Set aside.

2. **Date Filling:** Combine dates, water, and lemon juice in a 2-quart microwave-safe bowl. Microwave for 5 to 6 minutes at HIGH (100%). Stir well. Stir in marshmallows until partially melted.

3. Spread on crust. Cool at least 4 hours or overnight. Serve with whipped topping, if desired.

Yield: 16 to 24 bars.

❄

*Rotate dish, if necessary, for even cooking.

CARROT-RAISIN BARS

· · · · ·

TIPS

See page 9 for tips on shielding corners.

If you cannot use foil strips in your micro-wave oven, lower the power setting to ME-DIUM HIGH (70%) and increase the cook-ing time in step #2 to 8 to 9 minutes (total).

················ BARS ················

¾ cup flour

¼ cup butter or margarine

⅓ cup brown sugar, packed

⅓ cup sugar

2 medium eggs

½ teaspoon vanilla

½ teaspoon baking powder

½ teaspoon cinnamon

¼ teaspoon nutmeg

1 cup grated carrots

½ cup raisins

················ CREAM CHEESE FROSTING ················

3-ounce package cream cheese

2 tablespoons butter or margarine

1 tablespoon milk

2 cups powdered sugar

1. **Bars:** Combine all ingredients, except carrots and raisins, in a mixing bowl. Mix until well blended. Fold in carrots and raisins. Spread into a greased and sugared 8-inch square microwave-safe dish.

2. Shield the corners of the pan. Microwave for 4 minutes at HIGH (100%). Remove shielding. Microwave again for 2 to 2½ minutes at HIGH (100%). Cool; then frost.

3. **Cream Cheese Frosting:** In a 2-quart microwave-safe bowl, combine cream cheese, butter, and milk. Micro-wave for 40 to 60 seconds at MEDIUM HIGH (70%) to soften. Stir well. Add powdered sugar; beat until fluffy.

Yield: 16 bars.

———————— · ❄ · ————————

TIPS
....

For an old-fashioned butterscotch flavor, add 1 teaspoon burnt sugar flavoring or vanilla to the filling in step #2.

COCONUT CHEWS
· · · · ·

An easy moist bar recipe.

.... CRUST ....

1 stick (½ cup) butter or
  margarine, softened

½ cup brown sugar,
  packed
1 cup flour

.... CHEWY FILLING ....

2 medium eggs, beaten
1 cup brown sugar,
  packed

2 tablespoons flour
1¼ cups coconut, flaked
½ cup (2 ounces) chopped
  walnuts

1. **Crust:** Combine crust ingredients until crumbly using a fork, pastry blender, or food processor. Press into a 9-inch square microwave-safe baking dish. Microwave for 3½ to 4 minutes at HIGH (100%). Set aside.
2. **Chewy Filling:** Beat eggs and brown sugar in a 2-quart microwave-safe bowl until fluffy. Stir in flour and coconut. Microwave for 3 to 4 minutes at HIGH (100%), stirring once.
3. Spread filling over crust. Sprinkle with walnuts. Microwave for 1½ to 2 minutes at HIGH (100%) to set. Let stand 10 minutes. Sprinkle with powdered sugar and cut into bars.

Yield: 16 to 24 bars.

——————— · ❄ · ———————

GUMDROP BAR COOKIES

OR FRUIT BARS

———— · · · · · ————

¾ cup brown sugar, packed

½ cup butter or margarine

2 eggs, beaten

1 teaspoon vanilla

¼ teaspoon baking powder

¾ cup flour

½ cup rolled oats (quick or regular)

¾ cup sliced gumdrops or dried fruit bits

1. Microwave brown sugar and butter in a 2-quart microwave-safe bowl for 1 minute at HIGH (100%). Blend in eggs and vanilla.
2. Combine baking powder, flour, and rolled oats; add to brown sugar batter. Stir until well blended. Stir in gumdrops or dried fruit bits.
3. Spread into a greased and sugared 8-inch square microwave-safe dish. Shield corners with foil.
4. Microwave for 4 minutes at HIGH (100%).* Remove foil shielding. Microwave again for 1½ to 2½ minutes at HIGH (100%). Let stand 30 minutes. Sprinkle with powdered sugar or glaze with "Microwave Perfect" Glaze. (See page 148.)

Yield: 16 bars.

———— · ❄ · ————

TIPS
....

You can purchase pre-packaged dried fruit bits in the dried fruit section of your grocery store.

See page 9 for tips on shielding corners.

If you cannot use foil strips in your microwave oven, lower the power setting to MEDIUM HIGH (70%) and increase the time to 7 to 8 minutes (total) in step #4.

....

*Rotate dish once, if necessary, for even cooking.

See page 9 for tips on shielding corners.

If you cannot use foil strips in your micro-wave oven, lower the power setting to ME-DIUM HIGH (70%) and increase the total cooking time to 7 to 8 minutes in step #4.

.... BARS ....

½ cup raisins
¼ cup water
⅔ cup brown sugar, packed
⅓ cup butter or margarine, softened

½ teaspoon vanilla
2 medium eggs, beaten
Dash of salt
1 cup flour
½ teaspoon cinnamon
½ teaspoon baking soda

.... VANILLA CREME FROSTING ....

2 tablespoons butter or margarine
2 tablespoons milk

2 cups powdered sugar
1 teaspoon vanilla

1. **Bars:** Microwave raisins and water in a small microwave-safe bowl for 2 minutes at HIGH (100%). Set aside.
2. Combine remaining ingredients in a large bowl. Mix until well blended. Stir in raisins and water.
3. Spread into a greased and sugared 8 × 12-inch microwave-safe baking dish. Shield corners with foil.
4. Microwave for 4 minutes at HIGH (100%).* Remove foil shielding. Microwave again for 2 to 3 minutes at HIGH (100%). Cool completely. Frost.
5. **Frosting:** Microwave butter and milk in a 2-quart micro-wave-safe bowl for 1 minute at HIGH (100%), or until bubbly. Beat in powdered sugar and vanilla. Spread on cooled bars.

Yield: 24 to 36 bars.

· ❄ · ─────

*Rotate pan once, if necessary, for even cooking.

Age is mostly a matter of mind. If you don't mind, it doesn't matter.

CAROB-RAISIN BROWNIES

(CHOCOLATE-FREE)

——————— . . . . . ———————

Tastes like chocolate but hasn't an ounce!

⅓ cup carob powder

½ cup butter or margarine

½ cup brown sugar,
  packed

½ cup granulated sugar

2 medium eggs

1 teaspoon vanilla

Dash of salt

½ teaspoon baking
  powder

¾ cup flour

½ cup raisins

1. Microwave carob powder and butter in a 2-quart microwave-safe bowl for 1 minute at HIGH (100%). Stir in sugar, thoroughly. Blend in eggs and vanilla.
2. Combine remaining dry ingredients and add to carob batter. Stir until well blended. Add raisins; stir.
3. Spread into a greased and sugared 8-inch square microwave-safe baking dish. Shield corners with foil.
4. Microwave for 4 minutes at HIGH (100%).* Remove foil shielding. Microwave again for 1½ to 2 minutes at HIGH (100%), until top is no longer wet. Cool.
5. Frost, if desired, with Carob Frosting. (See page 153.)

Yield: 16 bars.

——————— · ❄ · ———————

This is the perfect treat for those who love chocolate but cannot eat it because of food allergies or the caffeine content.

Carob powder is similar to cocoa in appearance and can be found in the health food section of your grocery store.

Carob can be substituted for cocoa, yet it contains one-tenth the amount of fat, four times the calcium, and none of the caffeine of chocolate or cocoa.

(See page 9 for tips on shielding corners.)

TIPS

....

*Rotate dish once, if necessary, for even cooking.

To ensure easy re-
moval of the bars,
spray the baking dish
with a nonstick vegeta-
ble coating in step #1
before adding the crust.

After microwaving the
crust in step #1, the
crust will look firm but
not browned.

For a delicate crust, use
the powdered sugar;
for a butterscotch-fla-
vored cookie crust, use
the brown sugar.

FRESH FRUIT BARS
———— · · · · · ————

A delightful summer dessert!

···························· CRUST ····························

1 cup flour   1 stick (½ cup) butter or
¼ cup powdered sugar or   margarine, softened
  brown sugar, packed

···························· FILLING ····························

8-ounce package cream   3 tablespoons sugar
  cheese   1 tablespoon milk

···························· FRUITS ····························

1 nectarine, washed, and   1 small bunch grapes,
  sliced   washed
1 pint strawberries,   1 kiwi fruit, peeled and
  washed, with stems   sliced
  removed   Other fresh fruit (optional)

1. **Crust:** Using a pastry blender, food processor, or fork,
   combine crust ingredients until crumbly. Press into an 8-
   or 9-inch square microwave-safe baking dish. Microwave
   for 3½ to 4 minutes at HIGH (100%).*
2. **Filling:** Microwave cream cheese, unwrapped, in a small
   microwave-safe bowl for 50 to 60 seconds at MEDIUM
   HIGH (70%). Stir in sugar and milk. Spread over cooled
   crust.
3. Place rows of fruit over filling, alternating colors and
   kinds of fruit. Chill at least one hour. Cut into squares.

Yield: 16 bars.

———— · ❄ · ————

··

*Rotate dish once while microwaving, if necessary, for even cooking.

CHILLED LEMON PUDDING BARS

A delicious summer treat. Try the chocolate, butter pecan, or pistachio variations!

························· CRUST ·························

1½ sticks (¾ cup) butter
  or margarine
1½ cups flour

3 tablespoons sugar
1 teaspoon vanilla

························ LAYER #1 ························

8-ounce package cream
  cheese
1 cup powdered sugar

12 ounces whipped
  topping (4¾ cups),
  divided

························ LAYER #2 ························

2½ cups milk

6-ounce package lemon
  instant pudding mix

1. **Crust:** Microwave butter in an 8 × 12-inch microwave-safe baking dish for 1 to 1½ minutes at MEDIUM HIGH (70%), or until melted. Stir in flour, sugar, and vanilla. Mix until crumbly. Press mixture into bottom of baking dish to form crust. Prick with a fork several times. Microwave for 4½ to 5½ minutes at HIGH (100%), or until no longer doughy, rotating pan once. Set aside to cool.
2. **Layer #1:** Microwave cream cheese, unwrapped, in a 2-quart microwave-safe bowl for 1 to 2 minutes at MEDIUM HIGH (100%), until very soft. Stir in powdered sugar and 1 cup of the whipped topping. Spread over cooled crust.
3. **Layer #2:** In a small bowl, beat the milk and the lemon pudding for 1 minute. Spread over Layer #1.

This is the traditional pudding-bar dessert we've been making for years. It's even easier to make with the help of the microwave oven.

Be sure to use the *instant* pudding mix and *not* the kind that requires cooking.

Spray the pan with non-stick vegetable coating for easy removal of the bars.

4. Cover Layer #2 with the remaining whipped topping. Chill at least 2 hours. Cut into squares.

Yield: 16 to 24 bars.

───────── · ❋ · ─────────

Chocolate Bars: Substitute 6-ounce package instant chocolate pudding mix for the lemon pudding mix.

Butter Pecan Bars: Substitute 6-ounce package instant butter pecan pudding mix for the lemon pudding mix.

Pistachio Bars: Substitute 6-ounce package instant pistachio pudding mix for the lemon pudding mix. (Great for St. Patrick's Day!)

HOLIDAY BREADS AND MUFFINS

· ❄ ·

PINEAPPLE PECAN COFFEE RING

· · · · ·

Use your range and microwave oven (or convection microwave) as a team to make this delectable coffeecake!

1 stick (½ cup) butter or
   margarine
1 cup brown sugar,
   packed
8½-ounce can crushed
   pineapple
½ teaspoon cinnamon

¼ cup chopped
   maraschino cherries
   (optional)
½ cup chopped pecans (2
   ounces)
2 large (12-ounce) tubes
   refrigerated buttermilk
   biscuits

TIPS
· · · · · · · ·

This delightful holiday bread is a real time-saver using the micro-wave oven. With a conventional oven alone, it will require 50 minutes, but you can cut the time in half by using the microwave oven in combination with a conventional oven. The ring tastes like a yeast bread that you spent hours preparing.

Be sure to use brand-name biscuits; generic biscuits tend to taste salty. (I prefer Pillsbury, Big Country, or Hungry Jack.) Three 10-ounce tubes of biscuits can be substituted for the two large 12-ounce tubes.

Be sure to use an oven-safe and microwave-safe bundt pan.

For an Almond Butter Coffee Ring, omit the cinnamon and crushed pineapple. Substitute sliced almonds for the pecans.

If you have a convection microwave oven, use the convection microwave variation.

TIPS
. . . .

Cut proofing time by one-half to one-third by allowing bread to rise in the microwave oven.

\1. Microwave butter and brown sugar in a 1-quart microwave-safe bowl for 1½ to 2 minutes at HIGH (100%), until boiling. Stir to make a syrup.
2. Drain crushed pineapple. (Juice can be saved for another use or discarded.) Stir pineapple, cinnamon, cherries, and pecans into the brown sugar syrup.
3. Pour two-thirds of the syrup into the bottom of a microwave- and oven-safe bundt pan. Stand biscuits on edge around the pan. Cover top with remaining syrup, using a spoon to spread.
4. Preheat your conventional oven to 400°F. Bake ring for 20 minutes, then microwave for 5 minutes at MEDIUM HIGH (70%). Cool 5 minutes. Invert and serve.

Yield: 1 10-inch coffee ring.

——————— · ❄ · ———————

For Convection Microwave: Omit step #4. Low-Mix Bake (or Combination 2 or Code 2)* at 350°F. for 25 minutes. Cool 5 minutes. Invert and serve.

O L D - F A S H I O N E D   C H E R R Y
C O F F E E   B R E A D

———————— · · · · · ————————

A beautiful Christmas bread that looks and tastes as if it took hours to make! (Use your convection microwave or your conventional oven plus your microwave.)

¼ cup sugar
2 teaspoons cinnamon

2 loaves frozen bread
    dough, thawed
21-ounce can cherry pie
    filling

1. Combine sugar and cinnamon; set aside.
2. Roll out 1 loaf of dough to 12 × 18 inches. Spread dough

. . . .
*Use the convection microwave setting that corresponds to your oven.

with half of sugar-cinnamon mixture. Roll up jelly-roll style, tucking under ends to seal. Shape into a ring. Cut two-thirds of the way through the ring at 1-inch intervals. Gently place into a greased and sugared oven- and microwave-safe bundt pan. Cover with plastic wrap. **To raise:** Microwave for 1 minute at MEDIUM (50%). Let stand 15 minutes. Repeat.

3. Repeat step #2 with second loaf up to and including cutting; cover with plastic wrap and set aside.

4. Spread three-quarters of the cherry pie filling over the raised dough in the bundt pan. Top with second ring, turning each section on its side like a fan. Cover with plastic wrap. **To raise:** Microwave for 1 minute at MEDIUM (50%). Let stand 15 minutes. Repeat.

5. Top ring with remaining pie filling.

6. **For convection microwave:** Low-Mix Bake at 350° for 35 to 38 minutes (or Combination 2 or Code 2 for 38 minutes). Cool pan on a rack for 10 minutes. Invert onto a serving plate. (It's beautiful!) Drizzle, if desired, with "Microwave Perfect" Glaze. (See page 148.)

For a microwave and a conventional oven: Use a microwave- and oven-safe bundt pan that has been greased and sugared. Preheat your conventional oven to 350°F. Bake for 40 minutes, then microwave for 6 to 7 minutes at MEDIUM HIGH (70%). Let stand 10 minutes. Invert.

Yield: 1 10-inch coffee ring.

———————— · ❄ · ————————

You can speed-proof any yeast bread dough by placing it in a microwave-safe dish, covering with plastic wrap, and microwaving for 1 minute at MEDIUM (50%). Let the dough stand for 15 minutes and then repeat. If your microwave oven does not have MEDIUM (50%) power, microwave for 1½ minutes at DEFROST (30%) instead.

Three convection microwave settings are suggested. Choose the one that corresponds to the power setting on your convection microwave.

Be sure to use brand-name biscuits, because generic biscuits tend to taste salty. (I prefer Pillsbury, Big Country, or Hungry Jack.)

Rotate the pan once, halfway through the cooking time, if necessary for even cooking in your microwave oven.

CARAMEL ALMOND BREAKFAST RING

——————— · · · · · ———————

A very easy brunch idea.

½ stick (¼ cup) butter or margarine
½ cup dark brown sugar, packed
1 tablespoon frozen orange juice concentrate

½ cup sliced almonds
¼ cup quartered maraschino cherries
10-ounce tube refrigerated biscuits (not generic)

1. Microwave butter, brown sugar, and orange juice concentrate in a microwave-safe ring mold for 1 to 2 minutes at HIGH (100%), or until bubbly. Stir well. Sprinkle with almonds and cherries.
2. Cut each biscuit in half and arrange over almonds and cherries to fill ring.
3. Microwave for 5½ to 7 minutes at MEDIUM (50%).* Let stand 2 to 3 minutes. Immediately invert onto serving dish. Serve warm.

Yield: 1 8-inch ring

——————— · ❄ · ———————

···

*Compacts (or ovens without a MEDIUM setting): Microwave for 2½ to 3 minutes at HIGH (100%), rotating pan once for even cooking.

HOLIDAY BREAD CRUMBS, CROUTONS, AND MELBA TOAST

DRY BREAD CRUMBS

—————— · · · · · ——————

4 slices wheat or white bread (fresh)

1. Place bread on two layers of paper towels in microwave oven. Microwave for 3 to 4 minutes at HIGH (100%), turning over once. Let stand at least 2 minutes; crumble.

Yield: 1 cup dry bread crumbs.

—————— · ❄ · ——————

CROUTONS

—————— · · · · · ——————

1 stick (½ cup) butter or margarine
8 slices of bread, cut into 1-inch cubes, to make 8 cups
½ teaspoon each: garlic salt, onion salt, and parsley flakes
2 tablespoons Parmesan or Romano cheese, grated
(optional)

1. Microwave butter in a glass measure for 40 to 60 seconds at HIGH (100%). Set aside.
2. Place bread cubes in a shallow microwave-safe baking dish. Microwave for 5 minutes at HIGH (100%), stirring once.
3. Stir remaining ingredients into the melted butter. Drizzle butter over the bread cubes, tossing to coat. Microwave for 4 to 5 minutes at HIGH (100%), or until crisp, stirring twice. Croutons will become even crisper after cooling.

Yield: 7 to 8 cups.

—————— · ❄ · ——————

TIPS
········

Since many holiday recipes call for dry bread crumbs or croutons, make your own following these simple instructions.

Use a food processor to crumble the bread crumbs after microwaving.

For 4 cups croutons: Cut the recipe in half and microwave for half the recommended time.

. . . . .

6 very thin slices of bread, cut in half

1. Place bread on two layers of paper towels in microwave oven. Microwave for 3 to 4 minutes at HIGH (100%), turning over once. Let stand at least 2 minutes.

Yield: 12 pieces.

———— · ❄ · ————

IRISH SODA BREAD

. . . . .

2 cups whole wheat flour
1 cup white flour
⅓ cup brown sugar (dark brown works best), packed
1 teaspoon salt

1½ teaspoons baking soda
¼ teaspoon baking powder
¼ cup butter or margarine, softened
1⅓ cups buttermilk
½ cup raisins

1. Mix dry ingredients together in a bowl. Cut in the butter. Beat in buttermilk until a soft dough forms. Fold in raisins.
2. Put the dough into a greased 8 × 5-inch or 9 × 5-inch microwave-safe loaf pan or a microwave-safe bundt pan.* Place the pan on an inverted saucer in the microwave oven. Microwave for 9 to 10 minutes at MEDIUM HIGH (70%). Let stand 5 minutes before removing from pan. Cool and wrap tightly in a plastic bag to store or slice, toast, and enjoy!

Yield: 1 loaf.

———— · ❄ · ————

*If you use a loaf pan, shield the corners with 1½-inch foil strips for the first 6 minutes of microwaving to prevent them from overcooking.

TIPS

When my husband and I visited Ireland a few years ago, we fell in love with the Irish soda bread. This recipe is a microwave adaptation from a conventional recipe we brought back with us (the conventional recipe requires 50 minutes at 350°F.). This microwave version is more moist than the conventional recipe and tastes best when toasted.

To ensure that the bottom of the loaf will cook evenly, place the pan on an inverted saucer in the microwave oven so the microwaves will bounce off the floor of the oven and cook the bottom.

See page 9 for instructions on shielding.

COCONUT QUICK BREAD

. . . . .

A nice coffee bread!

1¾ cups flour
1 cup flaked coconut,
   lightly toasted (see Tips)
¾ cup sugar
½ teaspoon baking
   powder
½ teaspoon baking soda

½ teaspoon salt
⅓ cup milk
⅓ cup vegetable oil
2 medium eggs, slightly
   beaten
1 teaspoon coconut extract
1–2 tablespoons graham
   cracker crumbs

1. In a large bowl, combine flour, coconut, sugar, baking powder, baking soda, and salt. Make a well in the center of the mixture. Set aside.
2. In another bowl, mix milk, oil, eggs, and extract. Add liquid ingredients to well in dry ingredients, stirring just until moistened.
3. Grease bottom and sides of a 9 × 5-inch glass or microwave-safe loaf pan. Sprinkle with graham cracker crumbs. Pour batter into dish, spreading evenly. Place on inverted saucer in the microwave.
4. Microwave, uncovered, for 10 minutes at MEDIUM (50%).* † Rotate dish and microwave again for 2½ to 3½ minutes at HIGH (100%), or until surface is no longer doughy. Let stand 10 minutes. Turn bread out onto a dish and cool completely. Wrap tightly and store in the refrigerator at least 12 hours before slicing.

Yield: 1 loaf

* Rotate dish twice, if necessary, for even cooking.
† Compacts: Microwave for 9 to 10 minutes at HIGH (100%).

TIPS
. . . .

To keep the corners from overcooking even slightly, shield them with foil for half the microwaving time.

See page 9 for instructions on shielding.

To toast coconut: Microwave 1 cup flaked coconut on a paper plate or pie plate, for 4 to 5 minutes, at MEDIUM HIGH (70%) or until coconut starts to turn light brown, stirring every 1 minute. Coconut will continue to brown for 1 minute after microwaving.

This bread is delicious and beautiful when sliced and arranged attractively on a doily-lined serving tray. I like it as much as any banana nut bread I've ever tasted.

To keep the corners from overcooking even slightly, shield them with foil for half the microwaving time (7 minutes).

See page 9 for instructions on shielding.

Choose two large ripe bananas; peel and be sure to remove any brown spots.

For an even "quicker" quick bread: Prepare step #1 using a food processor. Add the ingredients and process in the order listed.

BANANA PECAN BREAD

———— · · · · · ————

Less than 15 minutes in the microwave; conventionally 1½ hours. What a savings!

1 cup brown sugar, packed	2 ripe bananas, mashed
⅓ cup vegetable oil	1 teaspoon baking soda
1 teaspoon vanilla	½ teaspoon salt
2 medium eggs, beaten	1¾ cups flour
¼ cup buttermilk	1 cup (4 ounces) chopped pecans
	2 tablespoons graham cracker crumbs

1. Beat brown sugar and oil together in a large mixing bowl. Beat in vanilla and eggs until well blended. Stir in buttermilk and bananas. Add remaining dry ingredients, except the graham cracker crumbs, mixing well. Stir in pecans.
2. Grease and dust an 8 × 4-inch or 9 × 5-inch microwave-safe loaf pan with the graham cracker crumbs until bottom and sides are coated. Pour batter into loaf pan. Set on an inverted saucer.
3. Microwave for 10 minutes at MEDIUM (50%). Rotate dish one-half turn. Microwave again for 3 to 4 minutes at HIGH (100%). Let stand 5 to 10 minutes. Invert onto a serving dish and cool. Wrap in plastic wrap and refrigerate overnight before slicing.

Yield: 1 loaf.

———— · ❄ · ————

No matter how they dress it up
 upon the grocer's shelf,
No bread can ever be as good
 as what you bake yourself.
O wondrous smell! Crisp, brown crust!
 O butter melting through!
And best of all, the happy thought,
 That this was baked by you!

HIGH-FIBER APPLE BRAN MUFFINS

— • • • • • —

Use your convection microwave or your conventional oven!

·················· MUFFINS ··················

2¼ cups high-fiber bran
  cereal
1¼ cups milk
3 tablespoons vegetable oil
1 large egg or egg
  substitute (¼ cup)
½ cup brown sugar,
  packed
¼ teaspoon salt

3 teaspoons baking
  powder
1¼ cups whole wheat
  flour
1 large Delicious apple,
  cored and coarsely
  chopped
½ cup raisins

·················· TOPPING (OPTIONAL) ··················

½ cup whole wheat flour
¼ cup white sugar
¼ cup brown sugar,
  packed

½ teaspoon cinnamon
½ cup butter or
  margarine, softened

1. **Muffins:** Using a food processor, blender, or electric mixer, combine cereal, milk, vegetable oil, and egg. Process a few seconds until well blended. Add brown sugar, salt, and baking powder; process again until well mixed. Blend in flour; fold in apple and raisins.
2. Pour batter into 15 muffin cups (in muffin pans) or custard cups that have been sprayed with vegetable coating.
3. **Topping:** Using a food processor or pastry blender, mix topping ingredients until crumbly. Sprinkle each muffin with the topping.
4. **For Convection Microwave:** Low-Mix Bake (or Combination 2 or Code 2) at 400°F. for 20 minutes for 1 pan or

These high-fiber bran muffins have been a great help to my family members who must be on high-fiber diets. They are delicious and provide 8 grams of dietary fiber per muffin.

Don't worry if you don't have a convection microwave. This recipe works just as well using your conventional oven.

You can reheat these muffins by microwaving them for 10 to 15 seconds per muffin at MEDIUM HIGH (70%). For example, six muffins will take 60 to 90 seconds at MEDIUM HIGH (70%). If your microwave oven does not have a 70% power, use HIGH (100%) for the shortest amount of time recommended.

For the high-fiber bran cereal, I like to use All-Bran Extra Fiber.

Three convection microwave settings are listed. Choose the one that corresponds with the power setting on your oven.

25 minutes for 2 pans (using the raised rack). Let stand for 10 minutes. Invert and cool.

For Conventional Oven: Preheat oven to 400°F. Bake for 25 to 30 minutes. Let stand for 5 minutes. Remove from cups (or pan) and cool.

Yield: 15 muffins.

————————— · ❄ · —————————

HONEY-GLAZED BLUEBERRY MUFFINS

————————— · · · · · —————————

···················· GLAZE ····················

3 tablespoons honey	2 tablespoons butter or margarine, softened

···················· MUFFINS ····················

4 tablespoons butter or margarine	½ cup milk
½ cup sugar	½ teaspoon vanilla
1 medium egg, beaten	1 cup fresh or ¾ cup well-drained, frozen blueberries, slightly thawed
1½ cups flour	
1½ teaspoons baking powder	

1. **Glaze:** Mix glaze ingredients until blended and set aside.
2. **Muffins:** Microwave butter in a 2-quart microwave-safe bowl for 25 to 30 seconds at HIGH (100%). Stir in sugar and egg until well blended. Beat in flour, baking powder, milk, and vanilla. Stir in blueberries.
3. Line six muffin cups in a microwave muffin pan or custard cups with two papers liners each. Fill each two-thirds

full. Microwave six for 1½ to 2 minutes at HIGH (100%).

4. Spread each muffin with 1 teaspoon glaze. Microwave again for 30 to 60 seconds at HIGH (100%), or until a toothpick inserted in the center comes out clean. Remove outside paper liner and cool. Repeat with remaining batter.

Yield: 12 muffins.

———————— · ❄ · ————————

SWEET HONEY APPLE MUFFINS
———————— · · · · · ————————

A great high-fiber treat!

·················· GLAZE ··························

3 tablespoons honey

2 tablespoons butter or margarine, softened

·················· MUFFINS ··························

1 cup milk
1 tablespoon lemon juice
2 cups bran cereal (like All-Bran)
⅓ cup vegetable oil
¼ cup honey
1 medium egg, beaten

1½ teaspoons baking powder
¼ teaspoon salt (optional)
1 cup flour (white or whole wheat or a blend of both)
1 large apple (Delicious), cored and coarsely chopped
¼ cup raisins (optional)

1. **Glaze:** Mix glaze ingredients until blended and set aside.
2. **Muffins:** Combine milk and lemon juice in a large mix-

If your honey has crystallized or hardened in the jar, simply remove the lid and microwave for 30 to 60 seconds at HIGH (100%). For small amounts (¼ cup or less), microwave for only 20 seconds.

ing bowl. Stir in bran cereal. Let stand 5 minutes. Stir in oil, honey, and egg. Mix and add dry ingredients. Fold in chopped apple and raisins (optional).

3. Line six muffin cups in a microwave muffin pan or custard cups with two paper liners each. Fill each ¾ full with the batter. Microwave six for 2½ to 3 minutes at HIGH (100%).

4. Spread each muffin with 1 teaspoon glaze. Microwave again for 30 to 40 seconds at HIGH (100%), or until a toothpick inserted in the center comes out clean. Remove outside paper liners and cool. Repeat with remaining batter.

Note: For two muffins: Microwave for 1 minute at HIGH (100%). Glaze. Microwave again for 10 to 20 seconds at HIGH (100%).

Yield: 12 to 14 muffins.

———————— · ❄ · ————————

HOLIDAY CAKES

· ❄ ·

*ROSH HASHANAH, HANUKKAH, AND
PASSOVER CAKES*

ROSH HASHANAH APPLE AND HONEY CAKE

· · · · ·

⅓ cup pareve margarine
⅔ cup sugar
1 large egg
⅓ cup honey
½ cup whole wheat flour
½ cup white flour
¾ teaspoon baking soda

1 teaspoon cinnamon
Dash nutmeg
½ cup chopped nuts
   (optional)
2 cups peeled shredded
   Delicious apple

1. Microwave pareve margarine in a glass custard cup for 15
   to 20 seconds at HIGH (100%) to soften. Using a food
   processor or electric mixer and mixing bowl, process/beat
   margarine and sugar until light and creamy. Beat in

TIPS

· · · · · · · ·

Eating honey at Rosh
Hashanah signifies the
hope for a sweet new
year.

Margarine or butter
may be substituted for
the pareve margarine,
if desired.

honey and egg. Add flours, salt, soda, and spices; process/beat until blended. Fold in nuts and apple.

2. Pour batter into an 8- or 9-inch round microwave-safe baking dish that has been sprayed with vegetable coating and dusted with sugar. Place on an inverted glass pie plate in the microwave oven.

3. Microwave uncovered for 10 to 12 minutes at HIGH (100%)* or until no longer doughy. Let stand 10 minutes covered loosely with waxed paper or plastic wrap. Cut into wedges and serve drizzled with Hot Honey Sauce.

Yield: 1 8- or 9-inch round cake.

———————— · ❊ · ————————

HOT HONEY SAUCE

¼ cup honey   1½ tablespoons hot tap water
¼ cup sugar

1. Combine honey, sugar, and water in a 2 cup measure. Microwave uncovered for 1 to 1½ minutes at HIGH (100%) until boiling and thickened. Serve warm over cake wedges.

TIPS
....

Be careful not to over-microwave this delicate cake or it will become dry. The top will still look moist after microwaving.

LEKACH FOR PASSOVER (HONEY CAKE)

1 stick (½ cup) pareve   ⅓ cup orange juice
  margarine   2 teaspoons grated orange
⅔ cup sugar   peel (optional)
½ cup honey   1 teaspoon cinnamon
3 large eggs   Dash ginger
1 cup cake meal   ½ teaspoon allspice
½ cup potato starch   ½ cup chopped nuts

....

*Rotate pan once during microwaving if necessary for even cooking.

1. Microwave margarine for 15 to 20 seconds at HIGH (100%) to soften. Using a food processor or electric mixer, process/beat margarine and sugar until light and creamy. Beat in honey and eggs. Add remaining ingredients except nuts; process until well blended. Fold in nuts.

2. Line the bottom of a 9 × 5-inch glass or microwave-safe loaf pan with waxed paper. Grease waxed paper and sides with vegetable oil and dust with sugar. Pour batter into pan: spread evenly. Place on an inverted glass pie plate in the microwave oven.

3. Microwave uncovered for 13 minutes at MEDIUM (50%). Rotate pan. Microwave again for 2 to 2½ minutes at HIGH (100%) or until no longer doughy. Let stand 10 minutes covered loosely with waxed paper. Invert, cool, wrap in plastic wrap, and store until needed. Serve sliced with Hot Honey Sauce (see page 65), if desired.

Yield: 1 9 × 5-inch cake.

———————— · ❄ · ————————

Use only the zest or outer layer of the orange and lemon peel. Avoid using any of the white, bitter pith beneath the zest.

The zucchini provides the special ingredient to make this a very moist cake.

HANUKKAH ORANGE CAKE
WITH RUM SAUCE

——————— · · · · · ———————

······················ TOPPING ·······················

1 teaspoon cinnamon   2 tablespoons sugar

······················· CAKE ·······················

1 cup vegetable oil
2 cups brown sugar, packed
1 orange (⅓ cup juice plus 1 tablespoon grated peel)
1 teaspoon grated lemon peel

3 large eggs
2⅔ cups flour
2 teaspoons baking powder
1 teaspoon cinnamon
½ teaspoon nutmeg
¼ teaspoon cloves
2 cups peeled grated zucchini

1. **Topping:** Grease a microwave bundt pan. Mix ingredients for topping. Coat greased pan with topping. Set aside.
2. **Cake:** Using a food processor or electric mixer, process/beat vegetable oil and brown sugar until smooth. Add orange juice, peel, and eggs; beat well. Add remaining ingredients; beat until well blended. Fold in zucchini. Pour into prepared pan. Place on an inverted glass pie plate in the microwave oven.
3. Microwave uncovered for 20 to 22 minutes at MEDIUM HIGH (70%) or until no longer doughy, rotating pan every 7 minutes. Let stand 10 minutes, covered loosely with waxed paper. Invert onto serving plate. Serve with hot Rum Sauce.

Yield: 1 bundt cake.

——————— · ❄ · ———————

RUM SAUCE

⅓ cup orange juice   ½ cup sugar
1 tablespoon lemon juice   ½ teaspoon rum extract

1. Combine juices and sugar in a 1-cup measure. Microwave for 1 to 1½ minutes at HIGH (100%) or until boiling and thickened. Stir in rum extract. Serve warm over cake.

CHRISTMAS SEASON CAKES

TUDE'S RICH AND ELEGANT CHOCOLATE CHIP DATE CAKE

1 cup hot water
1 teaspoon baking soda
1¼ cups (8 ounces)
   chopped dates
¾ cup margarine, softened
1 cup sugar
2 medium eggs

1 teaspoon vanilla
¼ teaspoon salt
2 tablespoons
   unsweetened cocoa
1½ cups plus 1 tablespoon
   flour
½ cup chopped pecans (2
   ounces)
1 cup (6 ounces) semisweet
   chocolate chips
½ cup sugar
Whipped topping to
   garnish (optional)

TIPS

One tablespoon rum can be substituted for the rum extract, if desired.

This moist cake is a family favorite adapted from a recipe our Aunt Tude has been making for decades in her conventional oven.

Adding the chocolate chips and pecans partway through the cooking time will prevent them from sinking to the bottom of the pan.

For a very moist and rich cake, substitute 1 cup softened butter for the ¾ cup margarine.

1. In a 1-quart microwave-safe bowl, microwave hot water for 1½ to 2½ minutes at HIGH (100%), until boiling. Stir in baking soda and dates. Set aside.
2. In a mixing bowl, cream margarine and 1 cup sugar. Beat in eggs and vanilla. Sift salt, cocoa, and flour into sugar and egg mixture and stir. Fold in dates and water until blended.
3. Grease and sugar a microwave bundt pan and then sprinkle with ¼ cup chopped pecans. Pour batter into the pan. Microwave for 4 minutes at MEDIUM (50%).
4. Mix remaining pecans, chocolate chips, and sugar. Sprinkle evenly over partially baked cake. Microwave for 8 minutes at MEDIUM (50%),* † then microwave again for 3 to 5 minutes at HIGH (100%), or until a toothpick inserted in the center comes out clean. Let stand 8 to 10 minutes. Invert. Serve garnished with whipped topping and a few chocolate chips, if desired.

Yield: 1 bundt cake.

———————— · ❄ · ————————

* Rotate dish twice, if necessary, for even cooking.
† **Compacts:** Microwave for a total of 9 to 11 minutes at HIGH (100%) in step #4.

YULE MOCHA FUDGE CAKE

A beautiful dessert—and what a time-saver!

· CAKE ·

18-ounce chocolate,
  chocolate fudge, or
  chocolate mint pudding-
  in-the-mix cake mix

3 large eggs, beaten
⅓ cup vegetable oil or as
  cake package directs
1 cup water or as cake
  package directs

· · · · · · · · · · · · · YULE FILLING (OPTIONAL) · · · · · · · · · · · · · ·

½ of 3-ounce package
  pistachio instant
  pudding mix (⅓ cup
  dry)
½ cup milk

2 tablespoons powdered
  sugar
1½ cups whipped topping
  (3¾ ounces)

· · · · · · · · · · · · · MOCHA FUDGE FROSTING · · · · · · · · · · · · · ·

¼ cup strong coffee
⅓ cup butter or
  margarine, sliced

1 cup (6 ounces) semisweet
  chocolate chips
⅓ cup powdered sugar

· · · · · · · · · · · · · · · · · · · GARNISH ·

Crushed peppermint candies

1. **Cake:** Prepare cake as directed on the package using the
   ingredients listed. Pour batter into a greased and sugared
   microwave bundt pan.
2. Set on an inverted saucer. Microwave for 10 minutes at
   DEFROST (30%).* Rotate pan one-half turn. Microwave

*Compacts: Microwave 11 to 14 minutes (total time) at HIGH (100%) in-
stead of Step #2. Rotate pan 2 to 3 times during cooking.

Yule Mocha Fudge
Cake takes less than 20
minutes to prepare and
microwave. The Yule
filling is a pretty and
tasty addition, but it
can be omitted to save
time.

For even more time
savings, you can omit
the Mocha Fudge
Frosting too, and sim-
ply top the cake with a
can of cherry pie filling.

The cake will test done
when a toothpick in-
serted near the center
comes out clean. A few
moist spots may ap-
pear on top of the
cake, but they will
evaporate later. If the
center starts to sink, microwave the cake 1
minute longer.

Always dust the bundt
pan with sugar instead
of flour for easy re-
moval.

again for 5½ to 7 minutes at HIGH (100%), until no longer doughy. Let stand 5 to 8 minutes; invert onto a serving plate. Cool and refrigerate.

3. **Yule Filling:** Beat ⅓ cup pudding mix, milk, and sugar for 1 minute. Fold in whipped topping. Set aside.

4. Cut around top third of chocolate cake. Remove and set aside. Scoop out a small 1-inch tunnel in and around remaining two-thirds of cake. Fill with Yule Filling. Replace top of cake.

5. **Frosting:** Microwave coffee and butter in a 2-cup glass measure for 1 to 1½ minutes at HIGH (100%), until butter is melted and coffee is very hot. Stir in chocolate chips until melted. Blend in powdered sugar until smooth and creamy. Drizzle over cake.

6. **Garnish:** Garnish with peppermint candies. Chill until serving time. (Note: Cake freezes well.)

Variation: Yule Filling is optional. Omit steps #3 and #4, if desired.

Yield: 1 bundt cake.

———————— · ❄ · ————————

OLD-FASHIONED FRUIT CAKE

Only 15 minutes in the microwave!

Apple juice can be substituted for the traditional brandy used in fruit cakes. The brandy helps to preserve a fruit cake.

The glaze can be omitted, if desired, and cake can be wrapped tightly in cheesecloth that has been dampened with brandy. Wrap again in foil and store in a cool place. This method will preserve your fruit cake for up to two months.

·············· CAKE ··············

¾ pound mixed candied fruit, chopped (1½ cups) (red and green cherries, citron, pineapple, etc.)

¼ pound (¾ cup) golden raisins

¼ pound (½ cup) chopped dates

¼ cup brandy

1 stick (½ cup) butter or margarine, softened

½ cup brown sugar, packed

1 teaspoon vanilla

3 medium eggs

3 tablespoons molasses

¾ cup flour

½ teaspoon baking powder

Dash of allspice

½ teaspoon nutmeg

¼ pound (1 cup) broken nuts (pecans, Brazil nuts, almonds, walnuts, etc.)

·············· GLAZE ··············

2 tablespoons corn syrup

1 tablespoon water

1. **Cake:** Mix fruit, raisins, dates, and brandy in a 1-quart bowl. Set aside.
2. Beat butter, brown sugar, and vanilla until fluffy in a large mixing bowl. Beat in eggs and molasses. Mix remaining dry ingredients together in a small bowl; beat into brown sugar mixture. Stir in brandied fruit and nuts. Pour into a greased and sugared microwave bundt or ring pan.
3. Place on an inverted saucer. Microwave for 15 to 18 minutes at MEDIUM HIGH (70%), until a toothpick inserted near the center comes out clean. Let stand 5 minutes. Invert onto foil. Cool.

4. **Glaze:** Microwave corn syrup and water in a small dish for 30 to 50 seconds at HIGH (100%), until boiling hard. Cool to lukewarm. Pour over cooled cake. Wrap tightly and securely with foil. Store in a cool place.

Yield: 1 fruit cake ring.

_____ · ❄ · _____

····· CAKE ·····

6 ounces (1 cup) dried fruit bits (assorted packaged chopped dried fruit)
½ pound (1¼ cups) candied fruit (red and green cherries, pineapple, etc.)
½ pound (1½ cups) whole, pitted dates

¾ pound (2½ cups) pecan halves or assorted Brazil nuts, whole almonds, walnuts, etc.)
½ cup flaked coconut
⅓ cup flour
1 cup sweetened condensed milk

····· GLAZE ·····

1 tablespoon brandy or apple juice

2 tablespoons light corn syrup
1 tablespoon water

1. **Cake:** Combine fruits, nuts, and coconut in a mixing bowl. Set aside. Combine flour and sweetened condensed milk in a small bowl until smooth. Stir milk mixture into fruit and nuts. Pour into a greased and sugared microwave ring or bundt pan. Place on an inverted saucer.
2. Microwave for 4 minutes at HIGH (100%). Rotate dish one-half turn. Press with the back of a spoon to pack.

For easy measuring, the approximate cup measurement of the candied fruit or nuts is given in parentheses.

Save a few candied red or green cherries to garnish the fruitcake. Cut the green cherries in fourths to resemble leaves and place 2 or 3 "leaves" around each red cherry half—either on the cake or around the serving tray.

The flavor of fruitcake always improves after a few days of cool storage.

Microwave again for 3 to 4 minutes at HIGH (100%), until no longer glossy. Invert onto foil or plastic wrap.

3. **Glaze:** Brush with brandy or apple juice to preserve.
4. Microwave corn syrup and water in a small dish for 30 to 50 seconds at HIGH (100%), until boiling hard. Cool to lukewarm. Pour over cooled cake. Store in a cool place or refrigerate several days, wrapped securely with foil.

Yield: 1 fruit cake ring.

———————— · ❄ · ————————

CHOCOLATE AND PISTACHIO CAKE

————— · · · · · —————

A nice cake that takes less than 20 minutes!

···················· CAKE ····················

18-ounce package yellow cake mix (without pudding)
3½-ounce package pistachio instant pudding mix
½ cup vegetable oil

¾ cup water
4 medium eggs
4 drops green food coloring

···················· CHOCOLATE SWIRL ····················

3 tablespoons cocoa or ½ cup chocolate ice cream syrup

···················· CHOCOLATE GLAZE ····················

¾ cup sugar
3 tablespoons butter or margarine

3 tablespoons milk
½ cup (3 ounces) semisweet chocolate chips

TIPS
········

Remember the "Watergate Cake" of the seventies? This is the microwave version.

If you need a fast yet beautiful cake for a bazaar, try this one—this is always the first to be sold.

For added flavoring, substitute orange juice for half the water.

The cake will test done when a toothpick inserted near the center comes out clean. A few moist spots may appear on the surface, but they will evaporate as the cake cools. If the center starts to sink, microwave the cake 1 to 2 minutes longer.

Always dust the bundt
pan with sugar instead
of flour for easy re-
moval.

1. **Cake:** Combine all cake ingredients in a large bowl. Beat for 2 minutes at medium speed. Pour half the batter into a greased and sugared microwave bundt pan.
2. **Chocolate Swirl:** Stir the cocoa into the remaining batter in bowl. Pour cocoa-batter into bundt pan. Swirl through the batter with a knife to create a marbled effect.
3. Set on an inverted saucer. Microwave for 9 minutes at MEDIUM (50%).* Rotate one-half turn. Microwave again for 4 to 5 minutes at HIGH (100%), until no longer doughy. Let stand 7 to 8 minutes covered with waxed paper. Invert immediately and cool.
4. **Chocolate Glaze:** Microwave sugar, butter, and milk in a 1-quart microwave-safe bowl for 2 to 3 minutes at HIGH (100%), or until mixture boils. Stir in chocolate chips until smooth. Cool slightly until thickened. Drizzle over cake.

Yield: 1 bundt cake.

———————— · ❄ · ————————

TIPS
....

To prevent the cherries
and nuts from sinking
to the bottom of the
batter, mix them with 1
tablespoon additional
flour before stirring
them into the batter.

This cake will test done
when a toothpick in-
serted near the center
comes out clean. A few
moist spots may ap-
pear on the surface,
but they will evaporate
as the cake cools. If the

QUICK CHERRY FUDGE CAKE
—————— · · · · · ——————

A fast and easy one-layer cake with little cleanup!

1 cup flour
1 cup sugar
½ teaspoon baking soda
3 tablespoons cocoa
½ teaspoon salt
¼ cup vegetable oil

1 teaspoon white or cider
   vinegar
1 teaspoon vanilla
⅔ cup water
½ cup chopped
   maraschino cherries
½ cup chopped walnuts (2
   ounces)

....

*Compacts: Microwave for 11 to 14 minutes (total cooking time) at HIGH (100%) in step #3. Rotate pan three times for even cooking.

1. Sift or mix dry ingredients together into a 9-inch square or round microwave-safe pan that has been greased and sugared.
2. Make three wells in the dry ingredients. Place oil, vinegar, and vanilla in each well, distributing evenly.
3. Pour water over all and blend thoroughly with a fork, but do not beat. Stir in cherries and walnuts.
4. Microwave for 7 minutes at MEDIUM (50%) and for 2½ to 3½ minutes at HIGH (100%).* † (Shield corners, if using a square pan, for the first 7 minutes of the microwaving time.) Cool.
5. Frost with Chocolate Chipper Frosting (see page 154) and decorate with halved maraschino cherries.

Yield: 1 9-inch square cake.

———— · ❄ · ————

center starts to sink, microwave the cake 1 minute longer.

(See page 9 for tips on shielding corners.)

* Rotate dish once, if necessary, for even cooking.
† Compacts: Microwave for 7 to 8 minutes at HIGH (100%) (total cooking time).

For Cranberry Nut Bread: Mix all the cranberry sauce into the cake batter. Microwave as directed. Omit the glaze and sprinkle with sugar or powdered sugar instead. Cut into thin slices and place on a doily-lined serving tray.

The cake will test done when a toothpick inserted near the center comes out clean. A few moist spots may appear on the surface, but they will evaporate as the cake cools. If the center starts to sink, microwave the cake 1 to 2 minutes longer.

Always dust the bundt pan with sugar instead of flour for easy removal.

HOLIDAY CRANBERRY CAKE
· · · · ·

·························· CAKE ·························

18-ounce package pudding-in-the-mix yellow or butter cake mix
⅓ cup vegetable oil
16-ounce can jellied cranberry sauce (reserve ¼ cup for glaze)

3 large eggs, beaten
2 tablespoons orange juice concentrate
2–3 drops red food coloring (optional)
½ cup (2 ounces) finely chopped nuts (optional)

·························· GLAZE ·························

¼ cup reserved cranberry sauce
1 tablespoon butter or margarine

1 tablespoon frozen orange juice concentrate
1½ cups powdered sugar

1. **Cake:** Mix cake mix as directed on the package using the above ingredients and stirring the nuts in last. Pour batter into a greased and sugared microwave bundt pan.
2. Set on an inverted saucer. Microwave for 11 minutes at DEFROST (30%). Rotate pan one-half turn. Microwave again for 5 to 7 minutes at HIGH (100%), or until no longer doughy. Let stand 5 minutes. Invert onto serving dish. Cool completely. Glaze.
3. **Glaze:** Microwave cranberry sauce, butter, and orange juice concentrate in a small microwave-safe bowl for 40 to 60 seconds at HIGH (100%) until melted. Stir in powdered sugar until smooth. Pour over cake.

Yield: 1 bundt cake.

——————— · ❄ · ———————

One thing worse than being a quitter is being afraid to make a start.

MOTHER'S DAY AND SPRINGTIME CAKES

EASY GLAZED LEMON AND POPPY SEED CAKE

——————— · · · · · ———————

If a few moist spots appear on the cake after cooling, simply sprinkle the surface with sugar and they will disappear.

You can omit the glaze or heat and drizzle it on the cake right before serving.

· CAKE ·

18-ounce package lemon pudding-in-the-mix cake mix

3 large eggs, beaten

1 cup water (scant) or as package directs

⅓ cup vegetable oil or as package directs

2 tablespoons poppy seeds (optional)

· GLAZE ·

2 cups powdered sugar

2 tablespoons lemon juice

1½ tablespoons water

1. **Cake:** Mix cake mix as directed on the package using the remaining cake ingredients. Stir in poppy seeds. Pour batter into a greased and sugared microwave bundt pan.
2. Set on an inverted saucer. Microwave for 10 minutes at DEFROST (30%). Rotate pan one-half turn. Microwave again for 5 to 7 minutes at HIGH (100%), or until no longer doughy. Let stand 5 to 7 minutes. Invert onto a serving dish. Cool completely. Glaze.
3. **Glaze:** Mix powdered sugar, lemon juice, and water in a small bowl until well blended. (Reserve half the glaze and refrigerate until serving time, if desired.) Pour remaining glaze over cake. (For a warm lemon-glazed cake, just before serving time, heat reserved glaze for 30 to 40 seconds at HIGH [100%]. Pour over cake or individual slices and serve.)

Yield: 1 bundt cake.

——————— · ❄ · ———————

In seeking happiness for others, you find it for yourself.

You can substitute 1 cup water for the can of pineapple in the cake. Use just ½ cup crushed pineapple (drained) for the frosting.

You can use up to twice as much coconut, if you like. For people who do not like coconut, the ½ cup used in this recipe can hardly be tasted (but it does help hold the frosting together).

Garnish the cake with additional maraschino cherries, if desired.

SELF-FROSTED TROPICAL FRUIT CAKE

A beautiful pineapple cake!

FROSTING

¼ cup butter or margarine
½ cup brown sugar, packed
½ cup coconut
½ cup (2 ounces) chopped pecans or walnuts

¼ cup chopped maraschino cherries
15¼-ounce can juice-packed crushed pineapple and juice

CAKE

18-ounce package yellow pudding-in-the-mix cake mix

⅓ cup oil
3 large eggs, beaten

1. **Frosting:** Microwave butter and brown sugar in a microwave bundt pan for 1 to 1½ minutes at HIGH (100%), until bubbly. Sprinkle with coconut, pecans, cherries, and ½ cup crushed pineapple, drained. Microwave again for 1 minute at HIGH (100%). Stir and spread evenly in pan. Cool.
2. **Cake:** Using a beater or electric mixer, beat cake mix, oil, and eggs for 1 minute at medium speed. Add remaining pineapple (with juice) and beat 1 minute longer. Pour batter over cooled frosting in the bundt pan.
3. Set on an inverted saucer. Microwave for 12 minutes at DEFROST (30%).* Rotate pan one-half turn. Microwave again for 7 to 8 minutes at HIGH (100%).
4. Let stand 8 to 10 minutes, but no longer. Invert and spread cake with any frosting remaining in pan.

Yield: 1 bundt cake.

* ❄ ·

*Compacts: Microwave for 12 to 15 minutes (total time) at HIGH (100%) instead of step #3. Rotate pan three to four times during cooking.

The milk of human kindness should not be bottled up.

SELF-FROSTED ORANGE
MARMALADE CAKE

• • • • •

Beautiful and perfect for a bazaar or guests!

················· FROSTING ·················

3 tablespoons butter or
margarine

2 tablespoons brown
sugar, packed

⅔ cup orange marmalade

⅓ cup shredded coconut

················· CAKE ·················

18-ounce package lemon
or yellow pudding-in-
the-mix cake mix

1 cup water

⅓ cup vegetable oil

3 large eggs, beaten

⅓ cup orange marmalade

½ cup (2 ounces) chopped
pecans or walnuts
(optional)

1. **Frosting:** Microwave butter in a greased and sugared microwave bundt pan for 30 to 40 seconds at HIGH
   (100%). Stir in brown sugar, marmalade, and coconut,
   spreading evenly.
2. **Cake:** Beat cake mix, water, oil, and eggs for 2 minutes.
   Fold in marmalade and nuts. Pour cake batter over marmalade mixture in the prepared pan.
3. Set on an inverted saucer. Microwave for 11 minutes at
   DEFROST (30%). Rotate pan one-half turn. Microwave
   again for 6 to 7 minutes at HIGH (100%) or until no
   longer doughy. Let stand 5 to 8 minutes and invert. Cool
   completely.

Yield: 1 bundt bake.

———— · ❄ · ————

Variation: Self-frosted Orange Pound Cake: Substitute
⅔ cup sour cream for ½ cup of the water. Microwave for 8
minutes at MEDIUM (50%) and 4 to 5 minutes at HIGH
(100%) in step #3.

················

When love adorns a home, other ornaments are a secondary matter.

Be sure to use name-
brand (or thick) mar-
malade; thinner mar-
malade does not set
up well in the frosting.

You can use up to
twice as much coconut
if you like. For people
who do not like co-
conut, the ⅓ cup used
in this recipe can
hardly be tasted (but it
does help hold the
frosting together).

This quick little coffee cake makes nice use of garden rhubarb. It also works well with frozen rhubarb.

To freeze extra rhubarb, simply rinse the stalks, slice, and freeze in freezer plastic bags of 4 to 5 cups each (no sugar is necessary).

To use frozen rhubarb in a recipe, thaw slightly first by microwaving the frozen bag for 2½ to 3 minutes at HIGH (100%). Try to use before it is completely thawed and drained of juices.

QUICK RHUBARB CAKE

——————— • • • • • ———————

A quick treat from garden rhubarb.

.... CAKE ....

¾ cup brown sugar, packed	½ cup milk
1 stick (½ cup) butter or margarine	½ teaspoon baking powder
1 large egg, beaten	¾ cup flour
1 teaspoon vanilla	1¾ cups raw rhubarb, finely sliced

.... TOPPING ....

3 tablespoons sugar	1 teaspoon cinnamon

1. **Cake:** Microwave brown sugar and butter in a microwave-safe mixing bowl for 1 minute at HIGH (100%). Blend in egg, vanilla, and milk. Combine baking powder and flour; stir into batter until well blended. Fold in rhubarb. Spread into a greased and sugared 8-inch round microwave-safe baking dish.
2. Microwave for 7 minutes at HIGH (100%).
3. **Topping:** Mix topping ingredients together in a small bowl. Sprinkle topping over microwaved cake. Microwave for 2 to 3 minutes longer at HIGH (100%). Let stand 10 minutes. Drizzle with "Microwave Perfect" Glaze, if desired. (See page 148.)

Yield: 1 8-inch round cake.

——————— • ❄ • ———————

Kindness is like a cat. When you give it away it usually comes back.

RHUBARB COFFEE BUNDT CAKE

A sweet and tender cake to share with family and friends!

····················· TOPPING ·····················

2 tablespoons sugar   1 teaspoon cinnamon

······················ CAKE ·······················

1 stick (½ cup) butter or   1 teaspoon vanilla
  margarine   1½ teaspoons baking
½ cup brown sugar,   powder
  packed   1¾ cups flour (part can be
½ cup granulated sugar   whole wheat)
1 extra-large egg or 2 small   2½ cups finely chopped
  eggs   rhubarb, mixed with ½
⅔ cup milk   cup sugar

1. **Topping:** Grease a microwave bundt or ring pan. Mix ingredients for topping. Coat greased pan with topping. Set aside.
2. **Cake:** Microwave butter in a 2-quart microwave-safe bowl for 30 to 40 seconds at HIGH (100%). Beat in sugar and egg until creamy. Stir in milk and vanilla. Add baking powder and flour, beating until smooth. Stir in sweetened rhubarb.
3. Spread batter evenly in prepared pan. Place on an inverted saucer. Microwave for 12 minutes at MEDIUM (50%). Rotate pan one-half turn. Microwave again for 6 to 7 minutes at HIGH (100%), until no longer doughy. Let stand 2 minutes. Invert immediately. Serve warm if desired with a dollop of whipped cream, sprinkle with powdered sugar, or drizzle with heated vanilla frosting.

Yield: 1 ring cake.

TIPS

Substitute up to ¾ cup whole wheat flour for part of the flour recommended.

Frozen rhubarb can be used in this recipe. Thaw it slightly first by microwaving a 2-cup package for 1 to 2 minutes at HIGH (100%). Try to use it before it is completely thawed and drained of juices.

To avoid a lumpy lemonade glaze, you may want to sift the powdered sugar before stirring in the lemonade concentrate. I sift powdered sugar only if it looks very lumpy as most of the lumps will stir out.

For Lemonade Poppyseed Cake: Add 3 tablespoons poppyseeds to the batter in step #1.

S W E E T   S U M M E R   L E M O N A D E   C A K E

.... CAKE ....

19-ounce yellow cake mix (without pudding)
3¾-ounce package instant lemon pudding mix

1 cup water
¾ cup vegetable oil
4 medium eggs

.... GLAZE ....

⅓ cup frozen lemonade concentrate (½ of 6-ounce can)

1 cup powdered sugar

1. **Cake:** Combine cake mix, pudding mix, water, oil, and eggs in a large bowl; beat 2 minutes. Pour into a greased and sugared microwave bundt pan.
2. Microwave for 12 minutes at MEDIUM (50%). Microwave again for 3¼ to 4½ minutes at HIGH (100%), or until a toothpick inserted near the center comes out clean. (Note: Top of cake will look very moist.) Let stand 5 to 10 minutes before inverting.
3. **Glaze:** Mix lemonade concentrate and powdered sugar in a bowl until smooth. Invert cake and poke toothpick holes all over the cake. Immediately pour lemonade mixture over the cake. Cool before serving.

Yield: 1 bundt cake.

————— · ❄ · —————

More important than length of life is how we spend each day.

SELF-FROSTED COOKIES AND CREME CAKE

(WITH CHOCOLATE CRUMBLE TOPPING)

— — — · · · · · — —

To ensure easy re-
moval of the cake from
the bundt pan, grease
the pan with shortening
and dust with sugar as
recommended. If you
dust the pan with flour
as for conventional
baking, the cake will
not easily come out of
the pan and a thin
layer will stick to the
pan.

.... TOPPING ....

3 tablespoons butter or
margarine
2 tablespoons granulated
sugar
¼ cup brown sugar,
packed

10 chocolate sandwich
cookies, finely crushed
to make ¾ cup crumbs
¼ cup maraschino
cherries, halved

.... CAKE ....

18-ounce package white
pudding-in-the-mix
cake mix

1¼ cups water or as cake
package directs
¼ cup vegetable oil or as
cake package directs
2 eggs or as cake package
directs

.... COOKIE CRUMBS ....

12 chocolate sandwich
cookies, coarsely
crushed

1. **Topping:** Microwave butter and sugars in a greased and
   sugared microwave bundt pan for 1 to 1½ minutes at
   HIGH (100%). Stir in cookie crumbs and cherries. Set
   aside.
2. **Cake:** Combine cake ingredients in a large bowl; beat for
   2 minutes at medium speed. Pour cake batter over topping in prepared pan.
3. **Cookie Crumbs:** Sprinkle batter with coarsely crumbled
   cookies. Swirl gently with a knife.

4. Place on an inverted saucer. Microwave for 11 minutes at DEFROST (30%). Rotate pan. Microwave again for 6 to 7 minutes at HIGH (100%). Let stand 2 minutes. Invert immediately. Garnish with additional cherries.

Yield: 1 bundt cake.

———————— · ❄ · ————————

Variation: Cookies and Creme Chocolate Cake: Substitute 1 chocolate pudding-in-the-mix cake mix for white cake mix. Use the amount of water, oil, and eggs the package directs.

LABOR DAY AND HARVEST TIME CAKES

DELICIOUS ZUCCHINI-APPLE CAKE

———————— · · · · · ————————

···················· COATING ····················

| 1 tablespoon sugar | 1 teaspoon cinnamon |

···················· CAKE ····················

1¾ cups flour	½ cup milk
1 cup sugar	¼ cup frozen orange juice
1 teaspoon baking soda	concentrate
Dash of nutmeg	¼ cup vegetable oil
1 teaspoon cinnamon	1 large egg

···················· FRUIT AND NUTS ····················

1 cup grated zucchini	½ cup (2 ounces) chopped
1 cup grated apple	walnuts (optional)
	½ cup raisins (optional)

1. **Coating:** Grease a microwave bundt pan. Combine sugar and cinnamon and coat pan with mixture.
2. **Cake:** Combine all cake ingredients; blend at medium speed for 2 minutes. Stir in fruit and nuts. Pour into prepared bundt pan.
3. Microwave for 13 to 15 minutes at MEDIUM HIGH (70%), or until a toothpick inserted comes out clean. Let stand 5 minutes. Invert. Cool. Drizzle with "Microwave Perfect" Glaze (see page 148).

Yield: 1 bundt cake.

——————— · ❄ · ———————

···················· VARIATIONS ····················

Zucchini Cake: Omit apple. Use 2 cups grated zucchini (total).

Apple Cake: Omit zucchini. Use 2 cups grated apple (total).

CREAMY PEACH OR APPLE COFFEECAKE

——————— · · · · · ———————

························· CAKE ·························

1½ cups sliced apples or peaches, peeled

3 tablespoons water

1½ cups yellow or yellow butter cake mix

½ stick (¼ cup) butter or margarine, softened

2 medium eggs

8-ounce carton sour cream

2 tablespoons sugar

························· TOPPING ·························

1¼ cups graham cracker crumbs

¼ cup brown sugar, packed

½ stick (¼ cup) butter or margarine

½ teaspoon cinnamon

Dash of nutmeg and cloves (optional)

TIPS
·······

You can substitute 1 9-ounce Jiffy cake mix for the 1½ cups of yellow cake mix.

You can substitute 1 16-ounce can of sliced peaches or apples, drained well, for the sliced fruit. Omit step #1.

Ten to 12 graham crackers will make 1¼ cups crumbs.

1. **Cake:** Combine apples or peaches and water in a 1-quart microwave-safe bowl. Microwave, uncovered, for 3 to 4 minutes at HIGH (100%), until soft. Drain; set aside.

2. Combine dry cake mix, butter, and one egg in a mixing bowl until well blended. Spread into a greased and sugared 8-inch round microwave-safe baking dish. Microwave for 3½ to 4 minutes at HIGH (100%). Arrange apple or peach slices over cake.

3. Combine one egg, sour cream, and sugar. Spread over apples or peaches.

4. **Topping:** Combine topping ingredients in a small dish. Sprinkle over sour cream. Microwave for 8 to 9 minutes at MEDIUM (50%). Serve warm.

Yield: 1 8-inch cake.

———————— · ❄ · ————————

Variation: Add ½ cup chopped nuts to the topping in step #3.

If you must strain your eyes, do it looking on the bright side.

There is no such thing as a woman without talent—it takes talent to be one.

MADELINE'S MOIST CHOCOLATE ZUCCHINI CAKE

.... CAKE ....

¼ cup milk
½ teaspoon lemon juice
1 stick cup butter or
    margarine
2 medium eggs
1 teaspoon vanilla
½ cup vegetable oil
1½ cups sugar
¼ cup unsweetened cocoa

2½ cups flour
½ teaspoon baking
    powder
1 teaspoon baking soda
½ teaspoon salt
½ teaspoon cinnamon
2½ cups grated zucchini
½ cup (3 ounces)
    semisweet chocolate
    chips

.... GLAZE ....

1 tablespoon plus 2
    teaspoons hot water
1 tablespoon white corn
    syrup

1 tablespoon vegetable oil
1 cup powdered sugar

1. **Cake:** Mix milk and lemon juice together in a small bowl and set aside.
2. In a small microwave-safe bowl, microwave butter for 30 to 40 seconds at HIGH (100%), or until melted; set aside.
3. In a large bowl, blend the eggs, vanilla, oil, sugar, milk mixture, and melted butter. Mix remaining dry ingredients together and add to the egg mixture, blending well. Stir in zucchini.
4. Pour batter into a greased and sugared microwave bundt pan or 8 × 12-inch baking dish, spreading evenly. Sprinkle with chocolate chips. Microwave for 12 to 13 minutes at MEDIUM (50%).* Rotate pan one-half turn. Micro-

....
*Compacts: Microwave for 11 to 14 minutes at HIGH (100%) instead of the total microwaving time in step #4, rotating pan twice for even cooking.

To ensure easy removal of the cake from the pan, grease the pan with shortening and dust with sugar as recommended. Do not dust with flour as in conventional baking.

If you use the 8 × 12-inch pan, shield the corners with foil for the first 12 minutes of cooking time to help keep the corners from overcooking even slightly. See page 9 for tips on shielding.

The cake will test done when a toothpick inserted near the center comes out clean. A few moist spots may appear on the surface, but they will evaporate as the cake cools.

wave again for 6 to 7 minutes at HIGH (100%), or until no longer doughy. Let stand 10 minutes. Invert bundt pan. Cool and pour glaze over cake before serving.

5. **Glaze:** Mix glaze ingredients and microwave 30 to 40 seconds at HIGH (100%), until smooth and warm.

Yield: 1 bundt cake or 8 × 12-inch cake.

—————— · ❄ · ——————

T I P S
....

Instead of arranging the apples over the cake in step #2, you can stir the apples (mixed with the cinnamon-sugar) directly into the batter before pouring into the baking dish in step #1.

L I T T L E   D U T C H   A P P L E   C A K E

————— · · · · · —————

·············· CAKE ··············

¾ cup flour
½ teaspoon cinnamon
½ teaspoon baking powder
¼ cup brown sugar, packed

½ cup granulated sugar
¼ cup vegetable oil
1 large egg, beaten
1 teaspoon vanilla

·············· TOPPING ··············

1½ cups peeled and thinly sliced apples (1 large)

¼ cup sugar
½ teaspoon cinnamon
Powdered sugar, or whipped topping or frosting to garnish (optional)

1. **Cake:** Combine the dry ingredients. Stir in the liquid ingredients until well blended. Pour into a greased and sugared 8- or 9-inch round microwave-safe baking dish. Set aside.

2. **Topping:** Mix thinly sliced apples with sugar and cinnamon. Arrange apples over batter.

3. Microwave for 10 to 11 minutes at HIGH (100%), until edges of cake pull away from the pan. (Top of cake will still appear moist.) Let stand 5 minutes. Dust with powdered sugar and serve warm with a dollop of whipped topping. Or cool and drizzle with Vanilla Buttercream Frosting or Cream Cheese Frosting (see pages 149, 152).

Yield: 1 8-inch round cake.

———————— · ❄ · ————————

SPEEDY PUMPKIN BUNDT

· · · · ·

·········· TOPPING ··········

2 tablespoons sugar	1 teaspoon cinnamon

·········· CAKE ··········

18-ounce package yellow pudding-in-the-mix cake mix	1 cup pumpkin (canned)
	1 teaspoon cinnamon
⅓ cup vegetable oil	¼ teaspoon nutmeg
3 large eggs	⅛ teaspoon cloves
⅓ cup sugar	½ cup raisins

1. **Topping:** Grease a microwave bundt pan. Mix ingredients for topping. Coat greased pan with topping. Set aside.
2. **Cake:** Combine remaining ingredients except raisins using a food processor or wooden spoon. Pour and spread batter evenly in prepared pan. Sprinkle raisins on top of batter. Swirl with a knife to blend slightly (but so raisins don't sink to the bottom of the pan).
3. Place on an inverted saucer. Microwave for 12 minutes at MEDIUM (50%). Rotate pan one-half turn. Microwave

TIPS
·······

Add ½ cup chopped walnuts and swirl with the raisins, if desired.

For a Spicy Pumpkin Bundt Cake: Substitute one 18-ounce spice cake mix for the yellow cake mix and omit the cinnamon, nutmeg, and cloves.

again for 4½ to 5½ minutes at HIGH (100%). Let stand 8 to 10 minutes. Invert immediately. Cool. Drizzle with Vanilla Buttercream Frosting or Cream Cheese Frosting (see pages 149–152).

Yield: 1 bundt cake.

——————— · ❉ · ———————

TIPS
....
You can substitute 1 tea-spoon cinnamon, ½ teaspoon nutmeg, ¼ teaspoon ginger, and ⅛ teaspoon allspice for 2 teaspoons pumpkin pie spice.

PUMPKIN BUNDT CAKE

A delicious homemade cake in less than 20 minutes.

················· CAKE ·················

1 cup pumpkin (canned or cooked)	¾ teaspoon baking powder
2 cups flour (half whole wheat, if desired)	2 teaspoons pumpkin pie spice
1½ cups brown sugar, packed	⅔ cup butter or margarine, softened
1 teaspoon vanilla	⅓ cup milk
1 teaspoon baking soda	4 medium eggs, beaten
	1 cup raisins (optional)

················· TOPPING ·················

2 tablespoons sugar	1 teaspoon cinnamon

1. **Cake:** Combine all cake ingredients, except raisins, in a large mixing bowl. Beat 2 minutes using an electric mixer. Stir in raisins. Set aside.
2. **Topping:** Combine topping ingredients in a small bowl; sprinkle into a greased microwave bundt pan. Shake pan and distribute until well coated.
3. Pour pumpkin batter into the prepared pan. Set on an

inverted saucer. Microwave for 12 minutes at MEDIUM (50%). Rotate pan one-half turn. Microwave again for 5 to 6½ minutes at HIGH (100%).

4. Let stand 10 to 15 minutes. Invert and frost or drizzle with Cream Cheese Frosting (see page 152).

Yield: 1 bundt cake.

---- · ❄ · ----

RAISIN AND PECAN BUNDT CAKE

---- · · · · · ----

1 package butter pecan or butter brickle pudding-in-the-mix cake mix
1 teaspoon walnut flavoring (optional)

21-ounce can raisin pie filling
3 large eggs
½ cup pecans (optional)

1. Grease and sugar a microwave bundt pan. Using a mixer, blend all the ingredients in a large bowl. Beat for 2 minutes. Pour into the prepared pan.
2. Microwave for 12 minutes at MEDIUM (50%) and again for 5 to 7 minutes at HIGH (100%). Let stand 5 minutes. Invert. Cool. Drizzle with "Microwave Perfect" Glaze or warmed Cream Cheese Frosting (pages 148, 152).

Yield: 1 bundt cake.

---- · ❄ · ----

Use the food processor for even more convenience: Grate the carrots first and then empty the processor bowl. Process the liquid ingredients in step #1. Add the dry ingredients in step #2; process. Stir in the carrots last.

"DELICIOUS" PINEAPPLE-CARROT BUNDT CAKE

·····

1½ cups sugar
1 cup vegetable oil
3 medium eggs, beaten
8 ounces crushed
  pineapple, drained
2 cups grated carrots
1 teaspoon vanilla
1½ cups flour
1 teaspoon baking powder

1 teaspoon baking soda
½ teaspoon salt
½ teaspoon nutmeg
1 teaspoon cinnamon
1 cup chopped walnuts or
  pecans (4 ounces)

1. In a large mixing bowl, and using an electric mixer, beat sugar, oil, and eggs until blended. Stir in pineapple, grated carrots, and vanilla; blend well. Set aside.
2. In another bowl, thoroughly combine flour, baking powder, soda, salt, nutmeg, and cinnamon. Add to carrot mixture; mix well. Stir in nuts. Pour into a greased and sugared bundt pan.
3. Set on an inverted saucer. Microwave for 12 minutes at MEDIUM (50%).* Rotate pan one-half turn. Microwave again for 4 to 5 minutes at HIGH (100%). Let stand 5 minutes. Drizzle with Cream Cheese Frosting (see page 152).

Yield: 1 bundt cake.

———————— · ❄ · ————————

....

*Compacts: Microwave at HIGH (100%) for 12½ to 15 minutes (total time) instead of step #3.

HOLIDAY CHOCOLATE CANDIES

· ❄ ·

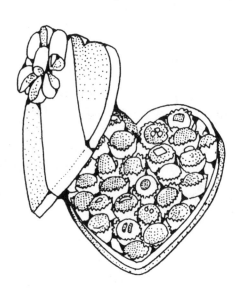

CHOCOLATE-COVERED CHERRIES

These taste heavenly!

·············· CENTER FILLING ··············

¼ cup solid white
   vegetable shortening

2 tablespoons milk
3 cups powdered sugar
1 teaspoon vanilla

TIPS

Maraschino cherries with stems are easier to dip and more fun to eat!

If you can keep these candies in your house for two or three days, the flavor gets even better and the centers turn to liquid. However, because they are delicious and are ready to eat in about an hour, they never last three days at our house.

A food processor works well, especially to quickly mix the filling.

Paraffin wax will *not* melt in a microwave oven, but when mixed with the chocolate chips, the heated chocolate causes the paraffin to melt. Be sure to grate the paraffin bar finely before adding it to the chocolate chips (a small hand grater works just fine).

.... CHERRIES ....

12-ounce bottle maraschino cherries, drained well (see Tip)

.... COATING ....

12 ounces (2 cups) semisweet chocolate chips

¼ cup grated food-grade edible paraffin

1. **Center filling:** Using a food processor or electric mixer, combine center filling ingredients. (Mixture will resemble pastry dough and may become stiff; knead by hand, if necessary [see tip].) Form into at least 30 balls. Pat each ball flat and wrap around a cherry. Place on waxed paper. Freeze until firm (at least 20 minutes).

2. **Coating:** Microwave chocolate chips and grated paraffin wax in a 2-quart microwave-safe bowl for 3 to 3½ minutes at MEDIUM HIGH (70%),* stirring twice. Stir until smooth. (If necessary, microwave again for 30 to 60 seconds at MEDIUM HIGH [70%]. Stir until smooth.)

3. Immediately, holding on to each stem or using tongs to hold cherries without stems, dip each cherry ball into the melted chocolate and place on a waxed paper–lined plate. Chill. Enjoy!

Yield: 30 candies.

———— · ❄ · ————

Variation: Chocolate-Covered Easter Eggs: Proceed with step #1 substituting whole almonds for the cherries or simply shape filling into 30 to 40 egg shapes about 1½" long. Place on waxed paper and freeze until firm. Proceed with steps #2 and #3 as directed above.

For colored eggs: White chocolate (such as Nestlé Ice Caps) or 12 ounces white almond bark can be substituted for

....

*Compacts: Use HIGH (100%) instead of MEDIUM HIGH (70%) for the same length of time in step #2.

the chocolate chips (omit paraffin if using the almond bark). Microwave at MEDIUM (50%) instead of MEDIUM HIGH in step #3. Add a small amount of paste food coloring to the almond bark to make the "colored" eggs.

SNOWCAPS
WHITE CHOCOLATE–COVERED CHERRIES WITH CHOCOLATE FILLING

—————— · · · · · ——————

·················· CENTER FILLING ··················

¼ cup margarine or
   vegetable shortening
⅓ cup unsweetened cocoa

2½ tablespoons milk
2⅔ cups powdered sugar
½ teaspoon vanilla

·················· CHERRIES ··················

12-ounce bottle
   maraschino cherries,
   drained well (use
   stemmed cherries for
   easiest dipping)

·················· COATING ··················

¾ pound (12 ounces)
   white chocolate*

¼ cup finely grated food-
   grade paraffin

1. **Center filling:** Using a food processor or electric mixer, combine center filling ingredients. (Mixture will resemble pastry dough and may become stiff; knead by hand if necessary.) Form into at least 30 balls. Pat each ball flat and wrap around a cherry. Place on waxed paper. Freeze until firm (at least 20 minutes).

···

*Substitute 1 pound (16 ounces) white almond bark for the white chocolate and paraffin, if desired.

TIPS
········

These delicious morsels taste even better if kept for two or three days before serving. The centers will turn to liquid after a day or two.

These candies freeze well for up to three months and can be kept in the refrigerator for up to two weeks.

Maraschino cherries with stems are found in the grocery store with bar supplies.

Look for white almond bark or white chocolate (like Nestlé Ice Caps) in the baking section of your grocery store (especially available in November and December).

2. **Coating:** Microwave white chocolate and grated paraffin in a 2-quart microwave-safe bowl for 3 to 4 minutes at MEDIUM (50%). Stir until smooth. (If necessary, microwave again for 30 to 60 seconds at MEDIUM [50%]. Stir until smooth.)

3. Immediately, holding on to the stem of each cherry or using tongs to hold stemless cherries, dip each cherry ball into the melted white chocolate and place on a waxed paper–lined plate. Chill and enjoy!

Yield: 30 candies.

———————— · ❄ · ————————

TIPS
········
When purchasing liqueurs, ask for Triple Sec (orange liqueur) or Chambord (raspberry liqueur).

S N O W C A P P E D   T R U F F L E S
WHITE CHOCOLATE–COVERED TRUFFLES

———————— · · · · · ————————

··················· **CENTER FILLING** ···················

¼ cup margarine or vegetable shortening

½ cup unsweetened cocoa

¼ cup orange or raspberry liqueur or juice

2½ cups powdered sugar

······················· **COATING** ·······················

¾ pound (12 ounces) white chocolate*

¼ cup finely grated food-grade paraffin

1. **Center filling:** Using a food processor or electric mixer, combine center filling ingredients. (Mixture will resemble pastry dough and may become stiff; knead by hand if necessary.) Form into at least 30 balls. Place on a waxed paper. Freeze until firm (about 1 hour).

···

*Substitute 1 pound (16 ounces) white almond bark for the white chocolate and paraffin, if desired.

2. **Coating:** Microwave white chocolate and grated paraffin wax in a 2-quart microwave-safe bowl for 3 to 4 minutes at MEDIUM (50%), stirring twice. Stir until smooth. (If necessary, microwave again for 30 to 60 seconds at MEDIUM [50%]. Stir smooth.)
3. Immediately, using tongs, dip each truffle into the melted white chocolate and place on a waxed paper–lined plate. Chill and enjoy.

Yield: 30 candies.

———————— · ❄ · ————————

MICROWAVE EASY CHOCOLATE TRUFFLES

————————— · · · · · —————————

A delicious after-dinner candy!

2 tablespoons butter or
   margarine
½ cup whipping cream
2 cups (12 ounces) milk
   chocolate chips

2 tablespoons orange
   liqueur or orange juice
¼ cup unsweetened cocoa
½ cup powdered sugar
½ cup chopped pecans
   (optional)

1. Microwave butter and whipping cream in a small microwave-safe bowl for 1 to 1¼ minutes at HIGH (100%), until hot. Set aside.
2. Microwave chocolate chips in a 2-quart microwave-safe bowl for 3 to 3½ minutes at MEDIUM HIGH (70%), until chips look very soft and shiny. (They will look soft but not melted.) Stir until smooth.
3. Stir cream into melted chips. Add liqueur; stir. Refrigerate until firm (about 3 hours).
4. Combine cocoa and powdered sugar in a small bowl. Set aside. Form chilled chocolate into 1-inch balls. Roll in cocoa mixture and then in pecans, if desired. Place on

TIPS
. . . .

Use real whipping cream in this recipe, but don't whip it.

For Raspberry Truffles: Substitute 2 tablespoons Chambord (or other raspberry-flavored juice or liqueur) for the orange liqueur.

For assorted truffles: Divide mixture in half after adding cream in step #3. Add 1 tablespoon orange liqueur to half the mixture and 1 tablespoon Chambord to the other half.

Instead of rolling truffles in the cocoa-sugar mixture, roll them in ½ cup chocolate-flavored decors (sprinkles).

waxed paper—lined plate or individual small fluted paper candy cups. Store in the refrigerator.

Yield: 24 candies.

—————— · ❋ · ——————

CHOCOLATE - TIPPED PRETZELS OR POTATO CHIPS

————— · · · · · —————

12 ounces (2 cups) semisweet chocolate chips
¼ cup finely grated food-grade paraffin

2–3 cups pretzels or ripple potato chips (sturdy ones)

1. Microwave chocolate chips and paraffin in a small microwave-safe bowl for 3 to 4 minutes at MEDIUM HIGH (70%). Stir until smooth.
2. Dip pretzels or potato chips in melted chocolate until partially coated. Gently shake off extra chocolate. Place on a waxed paper—lined plate and chill only until chocolate is set.

Yield: 2–3 cups.

—————— · ❋ · ——————

Variation: 16 ounces of chocolate or white almond bark can be substituted for the chocolate chips and paraffin. Melt 2 tablespoons vegetable oil with the almond bark.

TIPS
....

Use sturdy ripple potato chips for dipping in the chocolate. Regular chips will crumble and break from the weight of the chocolate.

. . . .

Never let a difficulty stop you . . . it may be the only sand on your track to prevent you from skidding.

CHOCOLATE - TIPPED STRAWBERRIES

· · · · ·

A delightful dessert or garnish for any holiday!

1 cup (6 ounces) semisweet
    chocolate chips
1 tablespoon vegetable
    shortening

1 pint large whole
    strawberries, washed
    with stems attached

1. Microwave chocolate chips and shortening in a small microwave-safe bowl for 1 to 1½ minutes at MEDIUM HIGH (70%). Stir until smooth.
2. Holding onto stems dip strawberries in melted chocolate until partially coated. Place on waxed paper–lined plate and chill until serving time (at least 15 minutes). Serve on colorful candy wrappers or cupcake liners or as a garnish on pies, cheesecakes, and so on.

Yield: 20 to 25 medium strawberries.

❄

TIPS
·········

I especially like to garnish individual servings of strawberry pie or Chocolate and Strawberries Truffle Pie (see page 182) with these tasty morsels.

The chocolate will stay firm at room temperature for about one hour so keep refrigerated until serving time.

CHOCOLATE PEANUT BUTTER BON-BONS

· · · · ·

3 cups crisp rice cereal or
    crushed corn flakes
1 pound (3¾ cups)
    powdered sugar*
18-ounce jar (2 cups)
    chunky or smooth
    peanut butter

1 stick (½ cup) butter or
    margarine
2 cups (12 ounces)
    semisweet chocolate
    chips*
¼ cup finely grated food-
    grade paraffin

·······································

*Substitute ¾ pound (12 ounces) chooclate almond bark for the chocolate chips and paraffin, if desired.

TIPS
·········

If chocolate becomes too firm while dipping, microwave again for 30 seconds at MEDIUM HIGH (70%). Repeat if necessary (add only 30 seconds at a time to prevent grainy chocolate, which can occur if the chocolate is overcooked).

1. Combine cereal and powdered sugar in a 2-quart mixing bowl. Set aside.
2. Microwave peanut butter and margarine in a 1-quart microwave-safe bowl for 1 to 2 minutes at HIGH (100%), or until melted. Stir. Pour this mixture over the cereal and mix well.
3. Form into 1-inch balls and chill or freeze at least 30 minutes.
4. Microwave chocolate chips and grated paraffin in a 1-quart bowl, uncovered, for 3 to 4 minutes at MEDIUM HIGH (70%),* or until chocolate chips look shiny and soft but not melted. (They will not look melted until stirred.) Stir until smooth.
5. Using a pair of tongs, dip each chilled ball into the chocolate, coating on all sides.
6. Place on waxed paper and let stand at room temperature until chocolate hardens.

Yield: 48 candies.

· ❄ ·

CHOCOLATE TURTLES

· · · · ·

Fun for the kids to make!

5 caramels
10–15 pecan halves, broken into smaller pieces

2-ounce cube chocolate almond bark

1. Microwave 5 caramels at a time on a piece of waxed paper for 40 to 60 seconds at DEFROST (30%), until soft but not melted. Shape each caramel to resemble a turtle shell. Stick broken pecan pieces in five places of each caramel to form a head and four legs of a turtle.

*Compacts: Use HIGH (100%) instead of MEDIUM HIGH (70%) for the same length of time in step #4.

2. Microwave 2 ounces of chocolate bark for 30 to 40 seconds at MEDIUM HIGH (70%) in a 1-quart microwave-safe bowl. Stir until smooth. (Be careful not to overcook chocolate. If not melted, microwave only 10 seconds longer, and then stir again.)
3. Spoon melted chocolate over the turtle bodies, leaving tips of pecans uncovered, or using tongs, dip entire turtle into melted chocolate. Place on waxed paper. Cool to set.

Yield: 5 candies per batch.

———————— · ❄ · ————————

CHOCOLATE PEANUT BUTTER SANDWICHES

——————— · · · · · ———————

A special treat for those who love Reese's Peanut Butter Cups. This is my husband's favorite candy!

1 cup creamy peanut
  butter
40 Ritz crackers

½ pound (8 ounces)
  chocolate almond bark

1. Spread peanut butter between 2 crackers to make a sandwich. Repeat to make 20 sandwiches.
2. Microwave chocolate bark in a 2-quart microwave-safe bowl for 2 to 3 minutes at MEDIUM HIGH (70%). Stir until smooth. If mixture is not smooth (melted) after stirring, microwave again for 30 seconds at MEDIUM HIGH (70%). Stir.
3. Using tongs, dip each peanut butter sandwich into the chocolate, coating on all sides. Place on waxed paper to harden. Enjoy!

Yield: 20 treats.

———————— · ❄ · ————————

TIPS
········

Never use HIGH (100%) power for melting chocolate unless you have a compact oven. In ovens of 500 watts or less, HIGH power is approximately equal in wattage to MEDIUM HIGH (70%) in a full-size microwave oven.

Variation: Mint Sandwich Treats: Substitute chocolate mint sandwich cookies for the peanut butter and Ritz crackers in step #1.

CHOCOLATE PEANUT BUTTER PEANUT CLUSTERS

½ pound (8 ounces) chocolate almond bark or white almond bark

⅓ cup creamy peanut butter

1½ cups (8 ounces) dry-roasted peanuts

1. Microwave almond bark and peanut butter in a 2-quart microwave-safe bowl for 2 to 3 minutes at MEDIUM HIGH (70%). Stir until smooth.
2. Stir in peanuts. Drop by teaspoonfuls onto waxed paper or into small fluted candy cups. Cool.

Yield: 24 candies.

❄

NUT GOODIE BARS

2 cups (12 ounces) butterscotch-flavored chips

2 cups (12 ounces) semisweet chocolate chips

1 cup creamy peanut butter

5 cups (10½-ounce bag) miniature marshmallows or 55 large marshmallows

½ cup salted peanuts

1. Microwave butterscotch chips, chocolate chips, and peanut butter in a 2-quart microwave-safe bowl for 3 to 4 minutes at MEDIUM HIGH (70%), stirring halfway

TIPS

I make this candy every year for the holidays. My guests love it, and I often send batches home with friends and family because it's so easy to make.

You can make this candy almost as fast as you can say "Chocolate Peanut Butter Peanut Clusters."

TIPS

If you are fond of peanuts, add up to ½ cup more peanuts in step #2.

through, until chips look soft and shiny (but not melted).
Stir until smooth.

2. Stir in marshmallow and peanuts. Spread evenly into buttered 9 × 13-inch pan. Cool 1 hour. Cut into bars. Store in the refrigerator.

Yield: 5 to 6 dozen bars.

————————— · ❄ · —————————

"THE BABE" BARS

1 cup sugar
1 cup light corn syrup
1½ cups creamy peanut
  butter
6 cups crispy rice cereal

1 cup (6 ounces)
  butterscotch-flavored
  chips
1 cup (6 ounces) semisweet
  chocolate chips

TIPS
....
"The Babe" Bars are named after the candy they resemble in taste.

1. Combine sugar and corn syrup in a 2-quart microwave-safe bowl. Microwave for 3 to 4 minutes at HIGH (100%), until boiling. Stir in peanut butter until well blended. Stir in cereal. Press into a 9 × 13-inch buttered pan. Set aside.

2. Microwave butterscotch chips and chocolate chips in 2-quart microwave-safe bowl for 3 to 3½ minutes at MEDIUM HIGH (70%), until they look soft and shiny. Stir until smooth. Spread over peanut butter and cereal bars. Cool. Cut into squares.

Yield: 5 to 6 dozen bars.

————————— · ❄ · —————————

· ·
*The only way to help people be what they want to be is to accept them
the way they are.*

TIPS
·······

Chocolate Peanut Butter Crispies and "The Babe" Bars require similar ingredients. The recipes differ mostly by what is done with the chips. For the "The Babe" Bars, the chips are melted and spread over the bars, while for the Chocolate Peanut Butter Crispies the chips are mixed into the bars. Both recipes are microwave versions of treats kids of all ages have been enjoying for years.

Peanut Butter Cap'n Crunch cereal works best in this recipe, although any crunchy cereal will work.

CHOCOLATE PEANUT BUTTER CRISPIES

· · · · ·
─────────────────

A favorite crispy rice treat for all kids!

1 cup sugar

1 cup light corn syrup

1 cup creamy or crunchy peanut butter

6 cups crispy rice cereal

1 cup (6 ounces) semisweet chocolate (or butterscotch-flavored) chips

1. Combine sugar and corn syrup in a 2-quart microwave-safe bowl. Microwave for 3 to 4 minutes at HIGH (100%) until boiling. Stir in peanut butter; mix well.
2. Add cereal and blend well. Stir in chips. Press into a 9 × 13-inch buttered pan. Cool. Cut into squares.

Yield: 48 bars.

───────── · ❄ · ─────────

BARB'S ALMOND BARK CRUNCH

· · · · ·

Too easy to taste so good!

1 pound (16 ounces) white almond bark*

2 tablespoons vegetable oil

3 cups crunchy cereal, especially the kind flavored with peanut butter

1. Microwave almond bark and oil in a 2-quart microwave-safe bowl for 3 to 4 minutes at MEDIUM HIGH (70%), or until it can be stirred smooth (melted).
2. Stir in cereal. Drop by tablespoonfuls onto waxed paper

···

*Chocolate almond bark can be substituted for the white almond bark.

and cool. Or spread onto a small cookie sheet. Cool to firm. Break the candy into pieces.

Yield: 24 to 36 candies.

— · ❈ · —

CHOCOLATE BAVARIAN MINTS

2 cups (12 ounces) semisweet chocolate chips
2 cups (12 ounces) milk chocolate chips
4 teaspoons butter

14-ounce can sweetened condensed milk
1 teaspoon vanilla
1 teaspoon peppermint extract

1. Microwave chips and butter in a 2-quart microwave-safe bowl for 3½ to 4½ minutes at MEDIUM HIGH (70%), stirring once, until chips look soft and shiny.
2. Stir until smooth. Add remaining ingredients and stir until blended. Pour into a buttered 9 × 13-inch pan. Refrigerate 1 to 2 hours, or until firm. Cut into squares. Store in the refrigerator.

Yield: 48 mints.

— · ❈ · —

PLANTATION CRUNCH BALLS

1 pound (16 ounces) chocolate almond bark
1 cup miniature marshmallows or 11 large marshmallows

3 cups crisp rice cereal
1 cup dry-roasted peanuts

TIPS

Chocolate Bavarian Mints freeze well for up to six weeks.

I like to use Rice Krispies in this candy because they maintain their "crispiness," which adds to the taste and texture.

1. Microwave almond bark in a 2-quart microwave-safe bowl for 3 to 4 minutes at MEDIUM HIGH (70%), stirring once, or until it can be stirred smooth.
2. Stir in remaining ingredients. Shape into 1-inch balls and drop onto waxed paper. Refrigerate for 1 to 2 hours until firm.

Yield: 4 to 6 dozen balls.

———————— · ❄ · ————————

TIN ROOF SUNDAE SQUARES
———————— · · · · · ————————

1 cup (6 ounces) semisweet chocolate chips
1 cup (6 ounces) cherry chips
14-ounce can sweetened condensed milk

2 cups miniature marshmallows or 22 large marshmallows
1 cup dry-roasted peanuts or raisins

1. Microwave chocolate and cherry chips in a 2-quart microwave-safe bowl for 2½ to 3 minutes at MEDIUM HIGH (70%), stirring once, until chips look soft and shiny.
2. Stir in milk until blended. Add marshmallows and peanuts. Stir. Pour into a buttered 9 × 13-inch pan. Refrigerate 1 to 2 hours, or until firm. Cut into squares.

Yield: 48 pieces, or 2 pounds.

———————— · ❄ · ————————

HOLIDAY FUDGE

· ❄ ·

OLD-FASHIONED FUDGE

· · · · ·

¾ cup milk

2 cups sugar

2 (1-ounce) squares
   unsweetened chocolate

Dash of salt

1½ teaspoons light corn
   syrup

2 tablespoons butter or
   margarine

1 teaspoon vanilla

¾ cup broken walnuts
   (optional)

1. Combine milk, sugar, chocolate, salt, and corn syrup in a
   2-quart microwave-safe bowl. Microwave for 3 minutes at
   HIGH (100%).
2. Stir. Microwave again for 8 to 9 minutes at HIGH
   (100%), until a soft ball (234°F.) forms when a small
   amount is dropped in cold water. (Check temperature by
   using a microwave candy thermometer or by inserting a
   conventional candy thermometer into the mixture at the
   end of the cooking time.)

TIPS
· · · · · · ·

If fudge doesn't set, it
may not have been
cooked enough (to
234°F.) or cooled
enough. If this hap-
pens, add ¼ cup milk,
stir, recook, and beat. If
fudge becomes too stiff
before pouring, knead
until soft and press into
the buttered pan.

For cooking time ac-
curacy, use a microwave
candy thermometer.

3. Immediately pour into an 8-inch metal pan and place the pan into a sink of cold water to speed cooling. Cool approximately 5 minutes until 110°F., without stirring. Return mixture to bowl.

4. Add vanilla. Beat vigorously until mixture becomes very thick and starts to lose its gloss. Add ¾ cup broken walnuts, if desired. Quickly spread into buttered 8-inch square pan. Garnish with walnut halves, if desired. Cool and cut when firm.

Yield: 36 pieces.

———————— · ❄ · ————————

TIPS
....

Make sure you use a butter or margarine that is solid at room temperature so that the fudge will set up.

For an even richer fudge: Substitute evaporated milk or half-and-half for the milk in step #1.

I think dry-roasted peanuts taste best in this fudge recipe.

EASY MICROWAVE FUDGE

————— · · · · · —————

2 (1-ounce) squares
 unsweetened chocolate
1 stick (½ cup) butter or
 margarine
¼ cup milk

1 teaspoon vanilla
1 pound (3½ cups)
 powdered sugar
1 cup (4 ounces) chopped
 nuts (optional)

1. Microwave chocolate, butter, and milk in a 2-quart microwave-safe bowl for 1½ to 2½ minutes at MEDIUM HIGH (70%),* until butter looks melted. Stir until smooth and chocolate is melted.

2. Stir in vanilla; beat in sugar gradually until mixture is smooth and creamy, but not crumbly. Stir in nuts, if desired.

3. Pour into a buttered 8-inch square pan. Chill to firm (20 minutes). Cut into squares.

Yield: 36 pieces.

————— · ❄ · —————

....
*Compacts: Substitute HIGH (100%) for MEDIUM HIGH (70%) in step #1.
....

Diplomacy is the ability to take something and act as if you were giving it away.

Variation: Substitute ½ cup cocoa for the chocolate. Beat cocoa in with the sugar in step #2.

MELLOW CHIP FUDGE

Quick, easy, and delicious!

2 cups sugar
¾ cup evaporated milk
3 tablespoons butter or
  margarine
1½ cups (9 ounces)
  semisweet chocolate
  chips

1 cup miniature
  marshmallows or 11
  large marshmallows
1 teaspoon vanilla
Dash of salt

1. In a 2-quart microwave-safe bowl, combine the sugar, milk, and butter. Microwave for 5 to 6 minutes at HIGH (100%), until mixture comes to a full rolling boil for 1 minute, stirring occasionally.
2. Stir in chocolate chips, marshmallows, vanilla, and salt. Keep stirring (2 to 3 minutes), until chips and marshmallows are melted and thoroughly blended.
3. Pour mixture into a buttered 8-inch square pan. Chill. Cut into squares after cooling.

Yield: 36 pieces.

Variation: Mellow Peanut Butter Fudge: Substitute 1½ cups (9 ounces) peanut butter chips for the chocolate chips.

TIPS

You don't have to microwave the chocolate chips in this recipe. The boiling sugar-milk-butter mixture will cause the chips to melt as you stir them into the mixture in step #2.

Be sure to use the milk chocolate chips instead of semisweet chocolate chips. This candy requires the milk chocolate's extra sweetness.

EASIEST PEANUT BUTTER–MELLOW FUDGE

———— · · · · · ————

2 cups (12 ounces) milk chocolate chips

1 cup peanut butter (chunky works well)

4 cups miniature marshmallows or 44 large marshmallows

1. Microwave chocolate chips and peanut butter in a 2-quart microwave-safe bowl for 3 to 4 minutes at MEDIUM HIGH (70%), stirring after 2 minutes. Stir until smooth.
2. Add marshmallows and blend well. Pour into a buttered 8- or 9-inch square pan. Refrigerate briefly until firm. Cut into squares.

Yield: 36 pieces.

———— · ❄ · ————

For Opera Fudge, use a microwave candy thermometer, if possible. Cooking time and temperature accuracy are very important for this recipe.

OPERA FUDGE

———— · · · · · ————

The traditional blond and vanilla-flavored fudge!

2 cups sugar

1 cup half-and-half

Dash of salt

1 tablespoon butter

1½ teaspoons vanilla

½ cup marshmallow creme

½ cup chopped candied cherries

1. Combine sugar, half-and-half, and salt in a large 5-quart microwave-safe bowl. Microwave for 4½ to 5 minutes at HIGH (100%), until mixture boils, stirring once. Stir.
2. Microwave again for 6 to 8 minutes at MEDIUM HIGH (70%)* (or until 235°F. on the candy thermometer).

···

*Compacts: Substitute HIGH (100%) for MEDIUM HIGH (70%) in step #2.

3. Stir in butter and cool to 110°F. without stirring (about 15 minutes at room temperature).

4. Add vanilla and beat vigorously until mixture begins to hold its shape. Add marshmallow creme and continue beating until mixture starts to lose its gloss. Quickly stir in cherries and pour into a buttered 8-inch square pan. Cool. Cut into squares.

Yield: 36 candies or 1¼ pounds.

———— · ❄ · ————

PENUCHE, OR "BROWN SUGAR FUDGE"

———— · · · · · ————

3 cups light brown sugar, packed
¾ cup milk
1 tablespoon butter
1 tablespoon light corn syrup
¼ teaspoon salt
1 teaspoon vanilla
1 cup (4 ounces) chopped pecans or walnuts

TIPS
. . . .

If possible, use an upright mixer when beating a cooked candy-syrup mixture. It often takes 5 to 10 minutes of beating for the syrup to lose its gloss. Hand mixers may become over-heated in that time or you may become tired of holding the mixer. Underbeaten candy will not hold its shape.

1. Combine brown sugar, milk, butter, corn syrup, and salt in a 2-quart microwave-safe bowl. Microwave for 8 to 10 minutes at MEDIUM HIGH (70%),* until mixture reaches the soft ball stage (or 234°F. on the candy thermometer). Cool to 120°F. (about 35 to 40 minutes at room temperature).

2. Add vanilla. Beat until mixture holds its shape when dropped from a spoon and begins to lose its gloss. Quickly stir in nuts. Immediately pour into a buttered 8- or 9-inch square pan. Cool. Cut into squares when cooled and firm.

Yield: 36 candies or 1¼ pounds.

———— · ❄ · ————

*Compacts: Substitute HIGH (100%) for MEDIUM HIGH (70%) in step #1.

OLD-FASHIONED PENUCHE SQUARES

· · · · ·

An adaptation from Magic Recipes, *an old NBC radio program.*

2 cups brown sugar,
  packed
½ cup water

½ cup sweetened
  condensed milk
½ cup (2 ounces) chopped
  nuts

1. Combine brown sugar and water in a 2-quart microwave-safe bowl. Microwave for 3 to 3½ minutes at HIGH (100%), or until boiling.
2. Stir in sweetened condensed milk. Microwave for 8 to 10 minutes at MEDIUM HIGH (70%),* or until mixture forms a soft ball when a small amount is dropped in cold water (240°F. on a candy thermometer).
3. Stir in chopped nuts. Beat until thick and creamy. Pour into an 8-inch square buttered pan. Cool. Cut into squares.

Yield: 36 squares.

———— · ❄ · ————

*Compacts: Substitute HIGH (100%) for MEDIUM HIGH (70%) in step #2.

BUTTERSCOTCH FUDGE

It tastes like a million dollars!

1 cup brown sugar,
  packed
2 cups sugar
⅔ cup evaporated milk
⅓ cup butter or margarine
2 cups (12 ounces)
  butterscotch-flavored
  chips

7-ounce jar marshmallow
  creme
1 teaspoon burnt sugar or
  maple flavoring
½ cup (2 ounces) chopped
  walnuts (optional)

1. In a 2-quart bowl, combine the brown sugar, sugar, evaporated milk, and butter. Microwave for 3½ to 4½ minutes at HIGH (100%), or until mixture boils. Stir.
2. Microwave again for 4 to 4½ minutes at MEDIUM HIGH (70%),* stirring twice.
3. Stir in butterscotch-flavored chips until they are melted.
4. Stir in marshmallow creme and flavoring. Fold in nuts, if desired.
5. Pour into a buttered 9 × 13-inch pan. Cool at least 15 minutes until firm. Cut into squares.

Yield: 4 to 6 dozen pieces.

———————— · ❄ · ————————

TIPS

Butterscotch Fudge is a variation of the popular Million-Dollar Fudge recipe.

For Million-Dollar Fudge: Substitute granulated sugar for the brown sugar and semisweet chocolate chips for the butterscotch-flavored chips. Be sure to microwave for 4 minutes beyond boiling.

*Compacts: Substitute HIGH (100%) for MEDIUM HIGH (70%) in step #2.

Be careful not to over-
cook the chips. The
mixture will not stir
smooth if you do.

Some brands of imita-
tion chocolate chips do
not melt in the micro-
wave, so be sure to use
real chocolate chips in
this recipe.

BUTTERNUT FUDGE

· · · · · ·

It's too delicious!

1 stick (½ cup) butter or
    margarine
1 cup smooth peanut
    butter
1 cup (6 ounces)
    butterscotch-flavored
    chips

1 cup (6 ounces) semisweet
    chocolate chips (not
    imitation)
2½ cups miniature
    marshmallows or 28
    large marshmallows
1 cup (2 ounces) dry-
    roasted peanuts

1. Place butter, peanut butter, and chips in a 2-quart microwave-safe bowl. Microwave for 2½ to 3½ minutes at
   MEDIUM HIGH (70%), stirring once. (Chips will look
   soft but not melted.) Stir well and chips will melt.
2. Stir in marshmallows and peanuts.
3. Pour into a buttered 12 × 8-inch dish.
4. Cool at least 30 minutes before cutting into bars.

Yield: 4 to 6 dozen pieces.

Any four-serving choc-
olate pudding mix
(*not instant*) works well
in this recipe.

Be careful not to over-
beat the cooked mix-
ture as the candy will
turn crumbly if you do.

EASY PUDDING FUDGE

· · · · · ·

Simply delicious and easy!

3½-ounce package
    pudding mix (not
    instant); use chocolate,
    fudge, or milk chocolate
    flavors

½ cup sugar
½ cup brown sugar,
    packed
⅓ cup milk
2 tablespoons butter or
    margarine

1. Combine pudding mix, sugars, and milk in a 2-quart microwave-safe bowl. Microwave for 4 to 5 minutes at MEDIUM HIGH (70%), until mixture comes to full boil, stirring once.
2. Continue to microwave for 3 minutes longer at MEDIUM HIGH (70%) while mixture is boiling.
3. Immediately stir in the butter. Beat with an electric mixer for 1 to 1½ minutes until slightly thickened. Pour into a buttered 9 × 5-inch loaf pan. Cool; cut into squares.

Yield: 24 squares.

· ❄ ·

Variation: Vanilla or Butter Pecan Fudge: Substitute 3½-ounce package vanilla or butter pecan pudding mix (noninstant) for the chocolate pudding mix.

PEANUT BUTTER FUDGIES

14-ounce can sweetened condensed milk, divided
½ stick (¼ cup) butter or margarine, divided
2 cups (12 ounces) peanut butter chips

½ cup (2 ounces) chopped peanuts
1 cup (6 ounces) semisweet chocolate chips

1. Microwave 1 cup sweetened condensed milk and 2 tablespoons butter for 3 to 4 minutes at MEDIUM HIGH (70%)* until almost boiling. Stir in peanut butter chips until they are melted. Stir in peanuts. Spread into a greased 8- or 9-inch square pan.
2. Microwave remaining sweetened condensed milk and butter for 2 to 3 minutes at MEDIUM HIGH (70%) until

*Compacts: Substitute HIGH (100%) for MEDIUM HIGH (70%) in steps #1 and #2.

almost boiling. Stir in chocolate chips until melted. Spread chocolate mixture on top of peanut mixture. Cool until firm. Cut into squares.

Yield: 24 squares.

———————— · ❄ · ————————

TIPS
....

Make this valentine treat for your special valentine!

VALENTINE'S SWEETHEART FUDGE

———————— · · · · · ————————

3 cups (18 ounces) semisweet chocolate chips
14-ounce can sweetened condensed milk

¾ cup (3 ounces) chopped dry-roasted peanuts or walnuts
½ cup coarsely chopped maraschino cherries

1. Lightly grease a 9-inch heart-shaped or square pan; line with waxed paper. Set aside.
2. Microwave chocolate chips in a 2-quart microwave-safe bowl for 5 minutes at MEDIUM (50%), or until chips stir smooth, stirring twice. Stir in milk until smooth. Add peanuts and cherries. Spread evenly into prepared pan. Chill two hours or until firm. Peel off waxed paper and cut into squares. Store in the refrigerator.

Yield: 2 pounds fudge.

———————— · ❄ · ————————

Variation: White Sweetheart Fudge: Substitute 1½ pounds (24 ounces) white almond bark or confectioner's coating for the chocolate chips. Proceed as directed.

HOLIDAY FAVORITE CANDIES

· ❄ ·

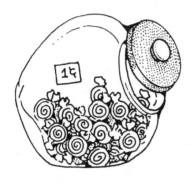

COCONUT CASHEW BRITTLE

· · · · ·

In less than 10 minutes makes a wonderful gift to share.

½ cup light corn syrup
1 cup sugar
1½ cup (6 ounces) dry-
   roasted cashews

1 teaspoon butter or
   margarine
1 teaspoon vanilla
½ cup shredded coconut
1 teaspoon baking soda

1. Combine corn syrup and sugar in a 2-quart microwave-safe bowl. Microwave for 4 minutes at HIGH (100%). Meanwhile, butter a large cookie sheet for use in step #4.

syrup in step #2 before microwaving. In step #3, just stir and continue to microwave.

2. Stir in cashews. Microwave again for 3 to 4 minutes at HIGH (100%), or until light brown.
3. Add butter, vanilla, and coconut. Blend well. Microwave again for 1 to 1½ minutes at HIGH (100%).
4. Add baking soda and gently stir until well mixed and foamy. Pour onto a large buttered cookie sheet. Cool 30 minutes. Break into pieces.

Yield: 1 pound candy.

———— · ❄ · ————

Variation: Old-Fashioned Peanut Brittle: Substitute 1 cup (4 ounces) dry-roasted peanuts for the cashews. Omit the coconut.

CHERRY MASH CANDY

· · · · ·

Delicious cherry chocolate peanut butter squares!

12 large marshmallows
2 cups sugar
Dash of salt
⅔ cup evaporated milk
1 stick (½ cup) butter or
  margarine
10-ounce package cherry
  chips

2 cups (12 ounces)
  chocolate chips (milk
  chocolate or semisweet)
⅔ cup creamy peanut
  butter
1 pound (4 cups) salted
  blanched or dry-roasted
  peanuts, chopped

1. Combine marshmallows, sugar, salt, milk, and butter in a 2-quart microwave-safe bowl. Microwave for 4 to 5 minutes at HIGH (100%),* until mixture boils. Microwave again for 4 minutes at MEDIUM (50%). Stir often.
2. Add cherry chips and stir until melted. Pour into a 9 × 13-inch buttered pan. Chill until firm.

*Compacts: Microwave for 6 to 8 minutes at HIGH (100%) instead of total time in step #1.

3. Combine chocolate chips and peanut butter in a 2-quart microwave-safe bowl. Microwave for 2 to 3 minutes at HIGH (100%). Stir until melted and smooth. Stir in peanuts.

4. Pour over cherry layer. Chill until firm. Cut into squares.

Yield: 4 to 5 dozen pieces.

———————— · ❄ · ————————

PRALINES MADE EASY

¾-ounce package butterscotch or vanilla pudding mix (not instant)

½ cup brown sugar, packed

1 cup sugar

5⅓-ounce can evaporated milk (½ cup plus 1 tablespoon)

2 tablespoons butter or margarine, softened

1 cup (4 ounces) pecan halves

1. Combine pudding mix, sugars, milk, and butter in a 2-quart microwave-safe bowl. Microwave for 8 to 9 minutes at MEDIUM HIGH (70%),* until mixture reaches soft ball stage (or 235°F. on a microwave candy thermometer), stirring three times.

2. Add pecans halves. Beat by hand for 2 minutes. Quickly drop by tablespoonfuls onto waxed paper about 2 inches apart. Let stand until firm. Store in a tightly covered container.

Yield: 24 candies.

———————— · ❄ · ————————

*Compacts: Microwave for 8 to 10 minutes at HIGH (100%) instead of MEDIUM HIGH (70%) in step #1.

¾ cup buttermilk
2 cups sugar
1½ (6 ounces) cups pecan
    halves

Dash of salt
2 tablespoons butter or
    margarine
1 teaspoon baking soda

1. Mix buttermilk, sugar, pecans, salt, and butter in a 5-quart casserole dish. Microwave for 11 to 13 minutes at HIGH (100%), or until a candy thermometer registers 235°F., stirring three times.
2. Stir in baking soda. (It will look foamy.) Microwave for 1 minute at HIGH (100%). Beat by hand for 1 to 2 minutes, until tacky to the touch. Drop by teaspoonfuls onto a sheet of waxed paper. Cool.

Yield: 15 to 20 candies.

Last week I looked for guests to come,
I kept my house so nice.
I scrubbed and cleaned till all was done,
Then dusted once, then twice.
Then at last, I gave my guests up
For they failed to appear.
Today I didn't wash one cup—
You guessed it! Guests are here!

SOUTHERN PRALINES

— • • • • • —

A traditional Southern favorite!

1 cup dark-brown sugar,
    packed
½ cup sugar
1 tablespoon butter or
    margarine

1 cup half-and-half
1 teaspoon vanilla
1 cup (4 ounces) pecan
    halves

1. Combine sugars, butter, and half-and-half in a 2-quart microwave-safe bowl. Microwave for 12 to 15 minutes at MEDIUM HIGH (70%), or until a candy thermometer registers 235°F. (the soft ball stage), stirring twice.
2. Add vanilla and pecans. Cool to 170°F. Drop by tablespoonfuls onto waxed paper. Let stand until firm. Store in an airtight container.

Yield: 10 3-inch pralines or 20 to 30 1-inch rounds.

———— • ❄ • ————

PEPPERMINT DIVINITY

— • • • • • —

A delicious variation of an old favorite!

2½ cups sugar
½ cup light corn syrup
½ cup water
Dash of salt
2 large egg whites
½ cup crushed candy
    canes or peppermint
    candy

¼ teaspoon peppermint
    flavoring (optional)
½ cup (2 ounces) chopped
    nuts
2–3 drops red food
    coloring (optional)

Use a microwave candy thermometer, if possible. Cooking time and temperature accuracy are very important for this recipe.

If possible, use an upright mixer to beat the syrup in step #4, because the beating will take 8 to 10 minutes. Hand mixers may overheat in that time and you may become tired of holding the mixer. Underbeaten divinity will not hold its shape.

You can use any chopped nuts in this recipe. I prefer to use walnuts.

1. Combine sugar, corn syrup, water, and salt in a 3-quart microwave-safe bowl. Cover with plastic wrap.
2. Microwave for 5 minutes at HIGH (100%). Stir.
3. Microwave again, uncovered this time, for 12 to 13 minutes at HIGH (100%), or until a hard ball forms when a small amount is dropped in cold water (or 258°F. on a candy thermometer).
4. Meanwhile, beat egg whites until very stiff. Pour cooked syrup over egg whites, beating constantly, until mixture starts to lose its gloss. (Note: It will usually require 8 to 10 minutes of beating with an electric mixer until candy loses its gloss.) Slowly beat in candy, flavoring, nuts, and food coloring (optional). (Divinity should hold its shape.) Drop by teaspoonfuls onto waxed paper. Cool.

Yield: 3 to 4 dozen candies.

——————— · ❄ · ———————

Variation: Old-Fashioned Divinity: Omit candy and substitute 1 teaspoon vanilla for the peppermint flavoring.

CHERRY DIVINITY

——————— · · · · · ———————

Or try other flavor variations!

½ cup hot water
⅔ cup light corn syrup
3 cups sugar
2 large egg whites

3-ounce package cherry gelatin, dry (or any other flavor)
½ cup (2 ounces) chopped nuts and/or ½ cup chopped candied cherries (optional)

1. Combine water, corn syrup, and sugar in a 3-quart microwave-safe bowl. Cover with plastic wrap. Microwave for 5 minutes at HIGH (100%). Stir.

TIPS
. . . .

Divinity requires at least 5 to 10 minutes of beating with an electric mixer before it will hold its shape. For best results, use an upright electric mixer (see tip for Peppermint Divinity on page 122).

You can use either ½ cup chopped nuts or ½ cup chopped candied cherries, or ½ cup of each.

2. Microwave, uncovered this time, for 12 to 15 minutes at HIGH (100%), or until a hard ball forms when a small amount is dropped in cold water (or 252°F. on the candy thermometer).

3. Meanwhile, beat egg whites until foamy. Add gelatin and continue beating until egg whites are stiff. Pour cooked syrup over egg whites, beating constantly, until candy will hold its shape. Fold in cherries or nuts, if desired. Drop by teaspoonfuls onto waxed paper. Cool completely and then store in an airtight container in a cool place.

Yield: 3 to 4 dozen candies.

———————— · ❄ · ————————

Variation: Substitute any flavor gelatin or candied fruit.

TIME-SAVING DIVINITY

———————— · · · · · ————————

There are no egg whites in this recipe!

7-ounce package fluffy
   white frosting mix
1/3 cup light corn syrup
1/2 cup warm water
1 teaspoon vanilla

1 pound (3¾ cups)
   powdered sugar
1 cup (4 ounces) chopped
   nuts and/or candied
   cherries and/or crushed
   peppermint candies

TIPS
········

Use either a Jiffy or Betty Crocker brand fluffy white frosting mix. The exact weight of the package will vary around 7 ounces.

1. Combine frosting mix, corn syrup, and water in a 2-quart microwave-safe bowl. Microwave for 2 to 3 minutes at HIGH (100%), until bubbly. Stir in vanilla and beat with a mixer for about 5 minutes until stiff peaks form.

2. Beat in powdered sugar. Stir in nuts and/or cherries and/or candies. Drop by teaspoonfuls onto waxed paper. Allow candy 6 to 12 hours to set.

Yield: 5 dozen candies.

———————— · ❄ · ————————

If taffy becomes sticky while you are pulling it, butter your hands lightly.

Enjoy a taffy pull at your next party: Make Saltwater Taffy ahead of time through step #3, pouring the mixture onto an 8-inch glass pan instead of the cookie sheet. (Cover loosely with plastic wrap and let stand until needed—up to one week.) At a party or other social event, reheat mixture by microwaving for 2 to 3 minutes at LOW (10%) to warm and soften. Butter hands and proceed with step #4 to pull taffy.

SALTWATER TAFFY

· · · · ·

1 cup sugar
¾ cup light corn syrup
1 tablespoon cornstarch
   dissolved in ⅔ cup
   water
2 tablespoons butter or
  margarine

1 teaspoon salt
3 teaspoons flavoring
  (strawberry, cherry, or
  your choice)

1. Combine sugar, corn syrup, cornstarch-water, butter, and salt in a 2-quart microwave-safe bowl. Cover with plastic wrap.
2. Microwave for 5 minutes at HIGH (100%). Stir. Microwave, uncovered, for 9 to 10 minutes at MEDIUM HIGH (70%), or until mixture reaches hard ball stage (258°F.).
3. Add flavoring; stir well. Pour mixture onto a buttered cookie sheet. Let stand 15 to 20 minutes to cool.
4. Pull taffy until it is satiny, light in color, and stiff. Pull taffy into long strips and twist, if desired. Cut into 2-inch pieces. Wrap with waxed paper or clear plastic wrap and store in tins.

Yield: 3 to 4 dozen candies.

———— · ❄ · ————

....
Laughter is the sunlight of the soul.

ENGLISH TOFFEE

— · · · · · —

1 stick (½ cup) butter or
  margarine
1 cup sugar
Dash of salt
4 tablespoons water

½ cup sliced almonds
4-ounce finely broken milk
  chocolate bar

1. Oil or butter the top 1 inch of a 3-quart bowl to prevent
   boilover. Place butter, sugar, salt, and water in the bowl.
   (Do not get sugar or salt on oiled top of bowl.)
2. Microwave for 10 to 12 minutes at HIGH (100%)
   (300°F.), or until lightly browned, stirring two times
   (with a clean spoon each time).
3. Spread almonds on a buttered 9 × 13-inch pan or cookie
   sheet. Pour cooked mixture over almonds.
4. Sprinkle finely broken chocolate bar over almond candy.
   Cool 5 minutes and gently spread melted chocolate over
   the candy with a spatula. Refrigerate until firm. Break
   into pieces to serve.

Yield: 36 pieces.

— · ❄ · —

OLD-FASHIONED TOFFEE

— · · · · · —

This is a delicious family favorite!

1½ cups (6 ounces)
  chopped walnuts or
  pecans
2 sticks (1 cup) butter or
  margarine

1½ cups brown sugar,
  packed
4 cubes (8 ounces)
  chocolate almond bark
  or 2 cups (12 ounces)
  semisweet chocolate
  chips

TIPS

· · · · · · · ·

Use a clean spoon every time you stir the toffee to prevent the formation of sugar crystals.

Instead of stirring with a clean spoon each time, you can leave a microwave-safe spoon in the toffee while it is microwaving and stir with it.

Always use a clean spoon every time you stir the toffee (see the tip for English Toffee).

1. Spread nuts in a buttered 9 × 13-inch pan. Set aside.
2. Combine butter and brown sugar in a 2-quart microwave-safe bowl. Microwave for 2 minutes at HIGH (100%). Stir until butter and brown sugar are completely dissolved.
3. Microwave again for 7 to 9 minutes at MEDIUM HIGH (70%), until mixture reaches 290°F. (soft crack stage), stirring two times (with a clean spoon each time).
4. Pour syrup mixture over nuts.
5. Microwave almond bark or chips in a 1-quart microwave-safe bowl for 2 to 3 minutes at MEDIUM HIGH (70%). Stir. Spread over toffee. Cool and enjoy!

Yield: 2 pounds candy.

———————— · ❄ · ————————

T I P S
....

If butterscotch chips do not stir smooth after microwaving in step #1, microwave again for 30 seconds at MEDIUM HIGH (70%) and stir. Repeat if necessary.

BUTTERSCOTCH YULE LOGS

———————— · · · · · ————————

2 cups (12 ounces) butterscotch-flavored chips
⅔ cup sweetened condensed milk

1 teaspoon vanilla
¾ cup chopped pecans

1. Microwave butterscotch-flavored chips in a 2-quart microwave bowl for 2½ to 3 minutes at MEDIUM HIGH (70%),* until they look soft and shiny (but not melted). Stir until smooth. Stir in milk and vanilla.
2. Chill until firm enough to roll. Roll into two log shapes, 1-inch thick. Roll in chopped pecans. Slice and serve.

Yield: 24 slices.

———————— · ❄ · ————————

....
*Compacts: Microwave for 2½ to 3 minutes at HIGH (100%) in step #1 instead of MEDIUM HIGH (70%).

TUDE'S EASY PEANUT BUTTER CANDY

———— · · · · · ————

An easy, nutritious treat that the kids can make in minutes!

½ cup light corn syrup
½ cup sugar
1 cup creamy or chunky
  peanut butter

2 cups crunchy cereal
  (corn flakes, Raisin
  Bran, Rice Krispies,
  etc.)

1. Combine corn syrup and sugar in a 2-quart microwave-safe bowl. Microwave for 2 to 3 minutes at HIGH (100%), until sugar is dissolved.
2. Stir in peanut butter. Add cereal and blend well. Drop by teaspoonfuls onto waxed paper. Cool to set.

Yield: 24 candies.

———— · ❄ · ————

PEANUT BUTTER PEANUT DROPS

———— · · · · · ————

1 cup sugar
½ stick (¼ cup) butter or
  margarine
¼ cup evaporated milk
¼ cup creamy peanut
  butter

1 teaspoon vanilla
1 cup rolled quick or
  regular oats
¾ cup (3 ounces) dry-
  roasted peanuts

1. Combine sugar, butter, and milk in a 2-quart microwave-safe bowl. Microwave for 2 to 3 minutes at HIGH (100%), until mixture boils. Stir.
2. Microwave again for 2 to 3 minutes at HIGH (100%).

3. Mix in peanut butter and vanilla. Stir in oats and peanuts. Drop by tablespoonfuls onto waxed paper. Let stand until firm.

Yield: 24 candies.

———————— · ❄ · ————————

CHRISTMAS MINTS

———————— · · · · · ————————

Great for showers, too!

3 tablespoons butter or
  margarine
3 tablespoons milk
14–15-ounce package
  vanilla frosting mix (dry)

1 teaspoon mint flavoring
  or to taste
3 drops green food
  coloring
Sugar

1. Microwave butter in a 1-quart microwave-safe bowl for 25 to 30 seconds at HIGH (100%). Stir in milk and frosting mix. Beat well with a spoon.
2. Microwave for 1 to 2 minutes at HIGH (100%), until bubbly. Add mint flavoring and food coloring. Stir. Cool 10 minutes.
3. Roll into small ½- to 1-inch balls. Dip into sugar and flatten with a fork dipped in sugar. Refrigerate or store mints in a plastic container between layers of waxed paper.

Yield: 48 mints.

———————— · ❄ · ————————

Variation: Tint mints yellow or peach, or pink for Mother's Day, bridal showers, and so on.

· ·
One of the most attractive things you can wear is a smile.

TIPS
· · · · · · ·
If mixture hardens too quickly in step #3 while you are forming the balls, simply microwave again for 25 to 30 seconds at HIGH (100%).

Any vanilla frosting mix works well for these mints.

POPCORN BALLS

(OR CHRISTMAS WREATHS OR TREES)

· · · · ·

2½ quarts popped corn
⅓ cup light corn syrup
⅓ cup water

1 cup sugar
½ stick (¼ cup) butter or
    margarine
Food coloring (optional)

1. For convenient cleanup: Place popped popcorn in a large, clean, double-ply grocery sack. Fold back and down on edges of sack, creating a cuff, so sack stands only 12 inches tall. Set aside.
2. Combine corn syrup, water, sugar, and butter in a 2-quart microwave-safe bowl. Microwave for 8 minutes at HIGH (100%). Stir.
3. Microwave again for 1½ to 3 minutes at HIGH (100%), until a firm ball is formed when a small amount is dropped in cold water (or 245°F. on a candy thermometer). Add a few drops food coloring.
4. Pour over popped corn; mix well; form into balls with buttered hands. Cool on waxed paper.

Yield: 8 to 12 medium balls.

———— · ❄ · ————

·················· VARIATIONS ··················

Christmas Wreath or Trees: Tint recipe with green food coloring. Shape into a wreath or trees. Decorate with gumdrops, red hots, or other candies.

Christmas Tree Ornaments: Make miniature wreaths, trees, and so on. Attach a pipe cleaner for a hook.

TIPS
·······

Pop the popcorn in a microwave corn popper or on the range or use microwave popcorn in a prepackaged bag. DO NOT pop the popcorn in a plain paper bag as that could result in a fire in your microwave oven.

When popping popcorn in the microwave, turn the oven off when popping slows to one to two seconds between pops. Do *not* expect all the kernels to pop. If you wait for that, the rest of the popcorn will scorch.

For Quick Caramel Apples: Microwave one 14-ounce package of caramels, unwrapped, and 2 tablespoons of milk in a 2-quart microwave-safe bowl for 3½ to 5 minutes at MEDIUM HIGH (70%), stirring twice. Using 6 small to medium apples and 6 sticks, proceed as directed in step #3.

You can substitute any unsweetened cereal for the crisp rice cereal. I like Kellogg's Rice Krispies best for this recipe because it maintains its crispiness.

For tips on melting chocolate see Notes on Chocolate, pages 21–22.

HOMEMADE CARAMEL APPLES

½ stick (¼ cup) butter or margarine

1 cup brown sugar, packed

¾ cup sweetened condensed milk

½ cup light corn syrup

1 teaspoon vanilla

6–7 sticks

6–7 apples, rinsed, dried, and stems removed

1. Microwave butter in a 2-quart microwave-safe bowl for 20 to 30 seconds at HIGH (100%), until melted. Stir in brown sugar, milk, and corn syrup.
2. Microwave for 12 to 13 minutes at MEDIUM HIGH (70%), until mixture reaches a firm ball stage (or 245°F. on a candy thermometer). Stir in vanilla. Cool slightly.
3. Insert sticks into apples. Dip each apple into caramel mixture. Coat lightly. Place on waxed paper to cool.

Yield: 6 to 7 caramel apples.

HOLIDAY CHOCOLATE ALMOND WEDGES (CANDY PIZZA)

2 cups (12 ounces) semisweet chocolate chips

8 cubes (16 ounces) white almond bark, divided

1 cup salted dry-roasted peanuts

1 cup miniature or 11 large marshmallows

1 cup crisp rice cereal

½ cup red maraschino cherries, chopped

½ cup green maraschino cherries, chopped

½ cup (2 ounces) slivered almonds or shredded coconut

1. Combine chocolate chips and 6 cubes (12 ounces) of the almond bark in a 2-quart microwave-safe bowl. Micro-

wave for 3½ to 4½ minutes at MEDIUM HIGH (70%),*
stirring twice. (Remember, the chips and bark will look
soft and shiny but not melted; they will look melted only
after stirring.) Stir until smooth.

2. Stir in peanuts, marshmallows, and cereal. Spread into a
buttered 12-inch pizza pan. Sprinkle red and green cherries and almonds over the chocolate-cereal mixture.

3. Microwave remaining 2 cubes (4 ounces) of white almond
bark in a microwave-safe bowl for 1 to 1½ minutes at
MEDIUM HIGH (70%).* Stir until smooth. Drizzle over
the mixture in the pan. Chill slightly until firm. Cut into
wedges. Enjoy!

Yield: 10 to 14 wedges.

———————— · ❄ · ————————

*Compacts: Substitute HIGH (100%) for MEDIUM HIGH (70%) in steps
#1 and #3. Use the same amount of time recommended.

HOLIDAY DESSERTS

TIPS

Frozen rhubarb can be substituted for the fresh rhubarb. To use frozen rhubarb, thaw slightly first by microwaving 4 cups (30 ounces) for 2½ to 3 minutes at HIGH (100%). Try to use frozen rhubarb before it is completely thawed and drained of juice.

QUICK RHUBARB CRISP
(WITH APPLE, PEAR, OR PEACH VARIATIONS)

4 cups fresh rhubarb,
  thinly sliced
1 cup sugar
2½ tablespoons flour

1½ cups (9 ounces) yellow
  butter or yellow cake
  mix (dry)
½ stick (¼ cup) butter or
  margarine, sliced
½ cup brown sugar,
  packed

1. Grease and sugar an 8- or 9-inch round microwave-safe baking dish. Mix rhubarb, sugar, and flour in the baking dish. Layer and crumble cake mix, butter, and brown sugar on top of rhubarb mixture.

2. Microwave for 11 to 12 minutes at HIGH (100%).* †
3. Let stand until completely cooled and chilled. (It will look very soft after cooking but will firm up after cooling or refrigerating.)

Yield: 12 servings.

———— · ❄ · ————

Variation: Quick Apple, Pear, or Peach Crisp: Substitute peeled and sliced fruit for the rhubarb. Reduce granulated sugar to 2 tablespoons and flour to 1½ tablespoons. Stir ½ teaspoon cinnamon and a dash of nutmeg into the fruit.

KATHY'S FRESH FRUIT PIZZA

·················· CRUST ··················

1 cup plus 2 tablespoons
  flour
⅓ cup brown sugar,
  packed, or powdered
  sugar

⅔ cup butter or
  margarine, softened

·················· FILLING ··················

11 ounces cream cheese (1
  8-ounce plus 3-ounce
  package)

⅓ cup sugar
2 tablespoons milk

·················· FRUITS** ··················

1 pint fresh strawberries,
  washed and stems
  removed
1 small bunch grapes,
  washed and separated

11-ounce can mandarin
  oranges, drained
1 kiwi fruit, peeled and
  sliced

*Rotate dish once, if necessary, for even cooking.
†Compacts: Microwave for 13 to 15 minutes at HIGH (100%) in step #2.

**You can use other fresh fruit, such as bananas, blueberries, pineapple, or peaches.

1. **Crust:** Using a food processor, pastry blender, or fork, combine crust ingredients until crumbly. Press into a buttered 10- or 12-inch microwave-safe pizza plate or serving dish. Form a fluted edge using your thumb and fingers. Microwave for 4 to 5 minutes at HIGH (100%). Set aside.

2. **Filling:** Microwave cream cheese, unwrapped, in a small bowl for 50 to 70 seconds at MEDIUM HIGH (70%), until very soft. Stir in sugar and milk. Spread over cooled crust.

3. **Fruits:** Attractively arrange fruits on filling. Place strawberries on outside, forming a ring; then form an inner ring with grapes; form another ring with oranges and place the sliced kiwi in the small center ring. Chill.

Yield: 1 12-inch dessert pizza

———————— · ❋ · ————————

Variation: Glazed Fruit Pizza: Brush fruit lightly with melted red currant jelly. (Microwave ¼ cup jelly for 60 seconds at HIGH (100%). Or brush with Fresh Fruit Glaze (see pages 147–148).

See pages 147–148.

See page 9 for shielding tips.

TIPS
········

If you cannot use foil strips in your microwave oven (check your owner's manual to be sure), use a lower power setting. For step #3, microwave for 6 minutes at MEDIUM (50%), rotate dish, and microwave again for 12 to 15 minutes at MEDIUM HIGH (70%).

EASY BUTTER BRICKLE PEACH
CRISP
———— · · · · · ————

29-ounce can sliced
 peaches in syrup
1 stick (½ cup) butter or
 margarine

18-ounce package butter
 brickle or butter pecan
 cake mix
½ cup brown sugar,
 packed

1. Grease and sugar an 8 × 12-inch microwave-safe baking dish. Empty peaches and syrup into the dish.
2. Microwave butter in a 2-quart microwave-safe bowl for 60 to 70 seconds at HIGH (100%), or until melted. Blend

in the dry cake mix until crumbly. Sprinkle over peaches. Sprinkle brown sugar on top. Shield corners with foil.

3. Microwave, uncovered, for 6 minutes at MEDIUM (50%). Rotate dish. Microwave for 5 minutes at HIGH (100%). Remove foil shielding. Microwave again for 4 to 5 minutes at HIGH (100%). Cool 2 to 3 hours to set.

Yield: 1 8 × 12-inch crisp.

———— · ❄ · ————

CHOCOLATE CHEESECAKE

1 cup (6 ounces) semisweet chocolate chips
2 tablespoons milk
3-ounce package cream cheese
3 tablespoons sugar

2 tablespoons milk
8 ounces (3½ cups) whipped topping
9-inch graham cracker pie crust (see page 187)

1. Microwave chocolate chips and 2 tablespoons milk in a 2-quart microwave-safe bowl for 1 to 1½ minutes at MEDIUM HIGH (70%). Stir until smooth.
2. Microwave cream cheese, unwrapped, in a small microwave-safe bowl for 30 to 40 seconds at MEDIUM HIGH (70%). Stir in sugar and milk. Quickly add to chocolate mixture. Beat well.
3. Fold in all but ½ cup whipped topping. Spoon into crust. Freeze at least 4 hours. Refrigerate 1 hour before serving. Serve garnished with reserved whipped topping and additional chocolate chips or curls, if desired.

Yield: 9-inch cheesecake.

———— · ❄ · ————

TIPS
....
This dessert is beautiful garnished with Chocolate-Tipped Strawberries. See page 100.

TIPS

Omit the pecans for a creamy filling.

CHOCOLATE PECAN CHEESECAKE

.... CRUST ....

1 stick (½ cup) butter or
  margarine
1 cup flour

3 tablespoons brown
  sugar, packed
½ cup chopped pecans

.... FILLING ....

½ cup semisweet
  chocolate chips
8-ounce package cream
  cheese
¼ cup brown sugar,
  packed
1 teaspoon vanilla

½ cup (2 ounces) chopped
  pecans
12-ounce (5¼ cups)
  container frozen
  whipped topping

1. **Crust:** Place butter in a 9-inch buttered microwave-safe pie plate. Microwave for 30 seconds at HIGH (100%), until melted. Stir in flour, brown sugar, and pecans. Spread evenly to form a crust. Microwave for 3½ to 4 minutes at HIGH (100%).
2. **Filling:** Microwave chocolate chips in a 2-quart microwave-safe bowl for 40 to 60 seconds at MEDIUM HIGH (70%). Stir until smooth. Add cream cheese and microwave again for 40 to 60 seconds at MEDIUM HIGH (70%), until chips and cheese are soft. Stir. Add sugar and vanilla. Stir thoroughly.
3. Fold in pecans and 3 cups whipped topping. Spread over crust. Freeze at least 4 hours.
4. Refrigerate 1 hour before serving. Spread with remaining whipped topping and serve sliced in wedges and drizzled with Quick Fudge or Praline Sauce, if desired (pages 157–158).

Yield: 1 9-inch cheesecake.

SWEET AND EASY BLENDER CHEESECAKE

———————— · · · · · ————————

···················· FILLING ·······················

8-ounce package cream
   cheese
2 tablespoons butter or
   margarine
½ cup milk
½ cup sugar

2 tablespoons flour
1 large egg
1 teaspoon vanilla

···················· CRUST ·······················

9-inch graham cracker
   crust in a microwave-
   safe pie plate (see page
   187)

1. **Filling:** Microwave cream cheese, unwrapped, and butter in a small microwave-safe bowl for 40 to 50 seconds at MEDIUM HIGH (70%) to soften. Pour into a food processor or blender. Add remaining filling ingredients. Process for 10 seconds or until thoroughly blended. Pour into the crumb crust.
2. Microwave for 5 to 6 minutes at MEDIUM HIGH (70%),* † or until center is almost set. Cool. Refrigerate until serving time. Serve garnished with Blueberry, Strawberry, or Raspberry Sauce (see pages 159–160) or cherry pie filling, if desired.

Yield: 1 9-inch cheesecake.

———————— · ❄ · ————————

*Rotate pie plate once halfway through microwaving time.
†Compacts: Substitute HIGH (100%) for MEDIUM HIGH (70%) in step #2.

TIPS
......

A prepackaged graham cracker crust makes this recipe even easier. However, if you want to make your own, see page 187.

LEMON AND CHOCOLATE SWIRL CHEESECAKE

.... **FILLING** ....

8-ounce package cream cheese

1 cup sugar

1 teaspoon vanilla

3 medium eggs, beaten

¼ cup lemon juice

.... **CRUST** ....

9-inch graham cracker crust (see page 187)

.... **SWIRL** ....

1 tablespoon butter or margarine

2 tablespoons unsweetened cocoa

.... **GARNISH** ....

4½ ounces (2 cups) whipped topping

1 small chocolate candy bar (2 ounces)

1. **Filling:** In a 1-quart microwave-safe bowl, microwave cream cheese, unwrapped, for 60 to 70 seconds at MEDIUM HIGH (70%). Stir in sugar, vanilla, eggs, and lemon juice; blend well.

2. Microwave for 6 to 8 minutes at MEDIUM HIGH (70%) until thickened, stirring three times. Reserve 3 tablespoons filling; pour remainder into graham cracker crust. Set aside.

3. **Swirl:** Microwave butter in a custard cup for 10 to 20 seconds at HIGH (100%), until melted. Stir in cocoa. Add reserved 3 tablespoons lemon filling; blend well. Drizzle over the filling in the crust. Gently swirl with a knife. Cover with waxed paper and refrigerate for 2 to 3 hours until chilled and firm.

4. **Garnish:** Serve topped with whipped topping and a piece of chocolate bar or a chocolate curl.

Yield: 1 9-inch cheesecake.

— · ❄ · —

DELICIOUS BREAD PUDDING

Serve with lemon sauce for a special treat.

·········· PUDDING ··········

2 cups milk
½ stick (¼ cup) butter or margarine
2 large eggs, slightly beaten
Dash of salt
½ cup brown sugar, packed

½ teaspoon burnt sugar flavoring (optional)
⅓ cup raisins
3 cups of ½-inch bread cubes

·········· LEMON SAUCE (OPTIONAL) ··········

1 tablespoon cornstarch
½ cup sugar
3 tablespoons melted butter or margarine

1½ tablespoons lemon juice
⅔ cup water
½ teaspoon grated lemon peel (optional)

1. **Pudding:** Microwave milk and butter in a 1-quart microwave-safe bowl for 2 to 3 minutes at HIGH (100%) or until butter is melted. Quickly beat in eggs until smooth. Stir in salt, brown sugar, flavoring, and raisins.
2. Arrange bread cubes in a 1½-quart casserole dish or 9-inch round microwave baking dish. Pour egg mixture over the bread cubes and toss lightly.

TIPS

For best results, use two- or three-day-old white, French or Italian bread.

You can substitute ½ teaspoon vanilla and a dash of cinnamon for the burnt sugar flavoring.

· · 140 · ·

3. Microwave for 10 to 12 minutes at DEFROST (30%),* or until center is almost set. Let stand 10 minutes. Serve warm with lemon sauce, if desired.
4. **Lemon Sauce:** Mix sugar and cornstarch in a 2-cup microwave-safe measure. Stir in butter and the remaining ingredients. Microwave for 2 to 3 minutes at HIGH (100%), or until boiling.

Yield: 6 servings.

———————— · ❄ · ————————

T I P S
· · · · · · · ·

You can also microwave Lemon Bread Pudding at HIGH (100%) in step #3. Place the casserole into another baking dish that has been filled with 1 cup hot water. Microwave for the same length of time.

L E M O N   B R E A D   P U D D I N G

——————— · · · · · · ———————

3 cups of ½-inch bread cubes	Dash of salt
2 cups milk	Dash of nutmeg
½ stick (¼ cup) butter or margarine	3 tablespoons lemon juice
2 large eggs, slightly beaten	½ teaspoon lemon flavoring or grated lemon peel
⅔ cup sugar	⅓ cup raisins

1. Soak the bread in milk in a bowl for 5 to 10 minutes.
2. Microwave the butter in a 1½-quart casserole or 9-inch microwave-safe baking dish for 30 to 40 seconds at HIGH (100%). Stir in the remaining ingredients, except the bread. Mix well. Add the soaked bread.
3. Microwave for 10 to 12 minutes of DEFROST (30%), or until center is almost set. Let stand 10 minutes. Serve warm or chilled.

Yield: 4 to 6 servings.

——————— · ❄ · ———————

· ·
*Compacts: Microwave for 12 to 15 minutes at DEFROST (30%) in step #3.

HOMEMADE VANILLA PUDDING

· · · · ·

Cooks in 7 minutes!

2½ tablespoons cornstarch	1 medium egg, beaten
Dash of salt	1 tablespoon butter or
½ cup sugar	margarine
2 cups milk	1½ teaspoons vanilla

1. Combine cornstarch, salt, and sugar in a 1-quart micro-wave-safe bowl. Stir in milk. Microwave for 5 to 7 minutes at HIGH (100%), stirring twice until slightly thickened.
2. Stir 2 tablespoons of this hot mixture into the beaten egg, stirring constantly. Add back into hot pudding and mix well. Microwave for 2 to 3 minutes at MEDIUM HIGH (70%), until thickened.
3. Add butter and vanilla. Pour into serving dishes and cool.

Yield: 4 to 5 servings.

* ❋ *

FLUFFY TAPIOCA PUDDING

· · · · ·

2 medium eggs, separated	Dash of salt, optional
2 cups milk	1 teaspoon vanilla
¼ cup sugar	2 tablespoons sugar
3 tablespoons tapioca	
(quick cooking)	

1. Combine egg yolks, milk, ¼ cup sugar, tapioca, and salt. Let stand 3 to 4 minutes.
2. Microwave for 5 to 8 minutes at HIGH (100%), or until boiling, stirring three times. Add vanilla.

For the holidays, tint pudding with a few drops of green food coloring and top with a cherry.

Fluffy Tapioca Pudding is delicious when served warm or chilled.

3. Beat egg whites until soft peaks form. Beat in 2 tablespoons sugar until well mixed. Fold tapioca mixture into egg whites. Spoon into serving dishes.

Yield: 4 to 6 servings.

———————— · ❄ · ————————

CREAMY RICE AND RAISINS

——————— · · · · · ———————

An old-fashioned recipe made easy—without a double boiler!

···················· PUDDING ····················

1 cup regular white rice (not quick), uncooked	½ cup raisins
4 cups milk	1 tablespoon butter or margarine
⅓ cup sugar	

···················· GARNISH ····················

1 tablespoon sugar	½ teaspoon cinnamon

1. **Pudding:** Combine rice, milk, and sugar in a 2-quart microwave-safe bowl. Cover with plastic wrap.
2. Microwave for 10 minutes at HIGH (100%), until very hot. Stir. Cover again.
3. Microwave for 25 to 30 minutes at DEFROST (30%). Stir in raisins. Cover again. Microwave for 5 to 8 minutes at DEFROST (30%), until liquid is absorbed. Stir in butter.
4. **Garnish:** Mix cinnamon and sugar together and sprinkle over rice to garnish. Let stand 5 minutes.

Yield: 6 servings.

——————— · ❄ · ———————

TIPS
·······

Be sure to leave a small edge turned back on the plastic wrap for a vent to help prevent a boilover. Venting plastic wrap also prevents a burst of steam from burning your hand when you remove the plastic wrap.

CHRISTMAS PLUM PUDDING WITH HARD SAUCE

• • • • •

Grandmother's recipe, adapted for the microwave.

½ cup very hot water
½ cup (4 ounces) chopped
  dates
1 cup flour
⅓ cup brown sugar,
  packed
½ teaspoon salt
1 teaspoon baking soda
2 medium eggs
1 stick (½ cup) butter or
  margarine, softened
⅔ cup orange juice
Dash of cloves

½ teaspoon cinnamon
¼ teaspoon nutmeg
6 slices white bread, crusts
  removed and cut into
  cubes to equal 4 cups
½ cup (2 ounces) chopped
  pecans or walnuts
  (optional)
½ cup (3 ounces) chopped
  candied cherries or
  candied pineapple
½ cup (3 ounces) currants

1. Combine hot water and dates in a small dish. Set aside.
2. Combine flour, brown sugar, salt, baking soda, eggs, butter, orange juice, cinnamon, nutmeg, and cloves using an electric mixer or food processor; beat or process until well blended. Add bread cubes, water, and dates; beat until blended. Fold in nuts, candied fruit, and currants.*
3. Pour batter into a microwave-safe bundt or ring pan that has been greased and dusted well with sugar. Cover with plastic wrap. Place on an inverted saucer in microwave.
4. Microwave for 14 to 17 minutes at MEDIUM (50%), or until pudding starts to pull away from edge of pan, rotating pan halfway through cooking time. Let stand, covered, for 10 minutes. Invert onto a serving plate. Serve warm with Hard Sauce (see following recipe). Pudding

. . . .

*Note: To prevent fruit and nuts from sinking to the bottom of the pudding, coat them with 2 tablespoons additional flour before folding them into the batter.

TIPS
. . . .

"The pudding was out of the copper. A smell like an eating-house and a pastry cook's next door to each other . . . Oh, what a Wonderful pudding! Bob Cratchit said that he regarded it as the greatest success achieved by Mrs. Cratchit since their marriage." —Charles Dickens, *A Christmas Carol*

I remember entering my grandma's farm house in O'Neill, Nebraska, and smelling the aroma of nutmeg, cloves, and cinnamon from all her Christmas baking. When Grandma Nora made plum pudding, after mixing the ingredients, she would meticulously and tightly wrap the pudding-batter in muslin. Then she would steam it for four hours over a kettle of boiling water on her wood-burning stove and turn it every 15 to 30 minutes with a long-handled spoon.

A lot of effort and love went into the plum pudding, but like the Cratchits, oh how we

• • 144 • •

loved it. Grandma never had a microwave oven, but I have her recipe, and this is the microwave version.

Grandma would be surprised to know that now it can be made in less than 15 minutes in the microwave oven.

can be reheated by microwaving individual servings for 15 seconds at HIGH (100%).

Yield: 1 ring.

———————— · ❄ · ————————

Variation: **Brandied Plum Pudding:** Reduce orange juice to ½ cup and add 3 tablespoons brandy with the orange juice in step #1.

HARD SAUCE FOR CHRISTMAS PUDDING
———————— · · · · · ————————

1 stick (½ cup) butter
1½ cups powdered sugar

1 teaspoon vanilla or 1 tablespoon lemon juice or 2 tablespoons brandy

1. Microwave butter in a 1-quart microwave-safe mixing bowl for 30 to 50 seconds at LOW (10%), or until soft, but not melted.
2. Using an electric mixer, beat the powdered sugar into the butter until creamy. Beat in the flavoring of your choice. Cover and refrigerate until needed.

HOLIDAY GRASSHOPPER CUPS
———————— · · · · ————————

A delicious after-dinner mint dessert.

TIPS
....

You can substitute 1¾ cups whipped topping for the whipped cream.

You can also substitute 1 teaspoon peppermint extract for the crème de menthe and crème de cacao.

If Grasshopper Cups are frozen, transfer them to the refrigerator

1½ cups (9 ounces) semisweet chocolate chips
3 tablespoons butter or margarine
1¼ cups miniature or 14 large marshmallows
⅓ cup milk

1½ tablespoons crème de menthe
1½ tablespoons crème de cacao
3 drops green food coloring
1 cup (8 ounces) whipping cream, whipped

1. Microwave chocolate chips and butter in a 2-quart microwave-safe bowl for 2½ to 3 minutes at MEDIUM HIGH (70%). Stir until smooth.

2. Line 10 2½-inch muffin cups with foil liners. Spoon 1 heaping tablespoon of the melted chocolate into each liner. Using a small soft brush, thoroughly coat the bottoms and sides of each liner with the chocolate. Refrigerate or freeze until firm (approximately 30 minutes or more).

3. Microwave marshmallows and milk in a 2-quart microwave-safe bowl for 2½ to 3 minutes at HIGH (100%), stirring once (marshmallows will look puffy). Stir until smooth. Stir in crème de menthe, crème de cacao, and food coloring. Refrigerate about 15 minutes or until the mixture is the consistency of egg whites. Fold in whipped cream.

4. Remove foil liners from chocolate cups. Spoon two heaping tablespoons of the marshmallow mixture into each chocolate cup. Refrigerate or freeze at least 4 hours. Serve garnished with additional whipped cream, a chocolate curl (shaved from a cube of almond bark), and a broken piece of peppermint candy cane.

Yield: 10 dessert cups.

———————— · ❄ · ————————

Variation: Holiday Grasshoper Cones: Proceed with step #1. Omit step #2; instead draw 10 4-inch circles on waxed paper, leaving space between circles. Spoon 1 heaping tablespoon chocolate mixture into each circle. Using the back of a spoon, spread chocolate to completely fill in each circle. Separate circles by cutting apart between spaces. Let stand 25 minutes at room temperature. Meanwhile, proceed with step #3. Omit step #4; instead, spoon 2 tablespoons whipped cream mixture into each circle. Bring up edges to form a cone shape. Refrigerate or freeze 2 hours; carefully peel off the paper. Serve or refrigerate or freeze until needed. Garnish as suggested in step #4.

30 to 40 minutes before serving time.

Store leftover cups in a tightly covered container in the freezer (up to 4 weeks).

HOLIDAY FROSTINGS AND GLAZES

· ❄ ·

TIPS

I like to make this glaze from juices drained from fresh or frozen strawberries. It is especially good drizzled over Fresh Fruit Bars (see page 49) or angel food cake.

FRESH FRUIT GLAZE

¾ cup fruit juice
   (pineapple, apple,
   orange, strawberry,
   pear, etc.)
1 tablespoon cornstarch

3 tablespoons sugar
1½ tablespoons crushed
   fruit or 1 teaspoon
   grated fruit rind
½ teaspoon appropriate
   fruit flavoring (optional)

1. Combine fruit juice and cornstarch in a 2-cup microwave-safe measure. Stir in sugar and crushed fruit or grated rind.
2. Microwave for 2 to 2½ minutes at HIGH (100%), stirring once, until mixture has thickened. Stir in flavoring.

Cool. Serve over fresh fruit, fruit salads, cakes, or bread puddings.

Yield: 1 cup glaze.

─────────── · ❄ · ───────────

"MICROWAVE PERFECT" GLAZE
─────────── · · · · · ───────────

Shiny, pretty, and delicious over cakes, bars, or rolls!

1 tablespoon plus 2 teaspoons hot water	1 tablespoon light corn syrup
1 tablespoon vegetable oil	1 cup powdered sugar

1. Mix liquid ingredients in a 1-quart microwave-safe bowl. Stir in powdered sugar.
2. Microwave for 40 to 50 seconds at HIGH (100%), until smooth and warm. Stir and pour over baked product. Serve immediately or cool and serve when glaze is set.

Yield: Glaze for 1 bundt cake or quick bread loaf.

─────────── · ❄ · ───────────

···················· VARIATIONS ····················

Lemon Glaze: Substitute lemon juice for water. Add ½ teaspoon finely grated lemon peel, if desired.

Chocolate Glaze: Add 2 tablespoons cocoa to powdered sugar.

· ·

You may live without books—what is knowledge but grieving;
You may live without hope—what is hope but deceiving;
You may live without love—what is passion but pining;
But where is the one who can live without dining.

TIPS
········

I use this glaze on almost any dessert because it gives such a pretty yet transparent look.

Before adding lemon peel, see the tip on page 40.

Orange Glaze: Substitute orange juice for water. Add ½ teaspoon grated orange peel, if desired.

Vanilla Glaze: Substitute 1 teaspoon vanilla for 1 teaspoon of the water.

VANILLA BUTTERCREAM
FROSTING

(WITH VARIATIONS)

————— · · · · · —————

······ LARGE BATCH (FOR TWO 8-INCH LAYER CAKES) ·······

1 stick (½ cup) butter or
  margarine
1 pound (3¾ cups)
  powdered sugar

Dash of salt
¼ cup milk or cream
1½ teaspoons vanilla

···················· SMALL BATCH (FOR ONE 8-INCH CAKE
OR PAN OF BARS OR BUNDT CAKE*) ·························

3 tablespoons butter or
  margarine
1½ cups powdered sugar

Dash of salt
2 tablespoons milk or
  cream
½ teaspoon vanilla

1. Microwave butter in a 2-quart microwave-safe bowl for 20 to 30 seconds at HIGH (100%), until very soft. Slowly beat in 1 cup powdered sugar (for the large batch or ½ cup for the small batch) and the salt until fluffy. Add remaining sugar, milk, and vanilla, blending until smooth.

Yield: Frosting for 1 or 2 8-inch layer cakes.

————— · ❄ · —————

*For bundt cake: Microwave the small batch of frosting for 20 to 30 seconds at HIGH (100%). Drizzle over cake.

Make one person happy each day—even if it's yourself.

TIPS

A food processor will make quick work for this frosting, but you can also use an electric mixer.

If you are planning to beat this frosting by hand (with a spoon), sift the powdered sugar first to remove any lumps.

You can add 1 to 2 teaspoons milk, after beating in step #1 to thin frosting, if desired.

Lemon or Orange Frosting: Omit vanilla. Stir in 1 teaspoon finely grated lemon or orange peel. Substitute lemon or orange juice for the milk.

Cherry Frosting: Stir in 2 to 3 drops red food coloring and 2 tablespoons chopped maraschino cherries.

Peanut Butter Frosting: Substitute creamy peanut butter for the butter. Add 1 tablespoon milk.

Chocolate Frosting: Increase butter to 4 tablespoons. Add 1-ounce square unsweetened chocolate. Microwave butter and chocolate for 30 to 40 seconds at HIGH (100%), or until very soft. Stir until smooth. Proceed as directed.

EASY WHIPPED CREAM FROSTING

No powdered sugar needed.

½ cup milk
1½ tablespoons flour
1 stick (½ cup) butter or
   margarine, softened

½ cup sugar
1 teaspoon vanilla

1. Combine milk and flour in a 1-quart microwave-safe bowl. Microwave for 1½ to 2 minutes at HIGH (100%). Beat with a mixer. Microwave again for 1 minute at HIGH (100%), or until thickened. Refrigerate to cool.
2. Using a mixer, beat remaining ingredients in a 1-quart mixing bowl until fluffy. Blend in cooled milk mixture. Frost any cooled cake.

Yield: Frosting for 1-layer or ring cake.

———————— · ❄ · ————————

Serving others is not so much a matter of occupaion as it is something within the heart that reaches out to others.

This delicious frosting tastes like bakery whipped cream frosting.

It's also the perfect frosting to "whip up" if you are out of powdered sugar.

For a two-layer cake, double the ingredients and microwave for 2 minutes at HIGH (100%) after beating in step #1.

You can substitute 1 teaspoon vanilla for the burnt sugar flavoring.

Fold 1 cup chopped raisins into the frosting with the flavoring to make an especially delicious frosting for carrot cake or German chocolate cake.

FLUFFY BROWN SUGAR FROSTING
———————— · · · · · ————————

½ cup brown sugar, packed
2 tablespoons water
¼ cup light corn syrup

2 large egg whites
1 tablespoon sugar
1 teaspoon burnt sugar flavoring (optional)

1. Combine brown sugar, water, and corn syrup in a 1-quart microwave-safe bowl. Cover with plastic wrap. Microwave for 3 minutes at HIGH (100%), or until boiling. Stir. Microwave, uncovered, for 2 to 2½ minutes at HIGH (100%), or until mixture reaches 242°F. (firm ball stage) on a candy thermometer.
2. Meanwhile, beat egg whites in a large mixing bowl until they stand in soft peaks; add sugar. Beat until stiff peaks form.
3. Pour brown sugar syrup slowly over egg whites, beating constantly until thick and fluffy. Blend in flavoring, if desired.

Yield: Frosting for 1 bundt cake or 8 × 12-inch pan of bars.

———————— · ❄ · ————————

Variation: For White Mountain Frosting: Substitute ½ white sugar for the brown sugar and proceed as directed.

CREAM CHEESE FROSTING

·············· **FOR 9×13-INCH CAKE OR BARS** ··············

8-ounce package cream   2 cups powdered sugar
  cheese   1½ teaspoons vanilla
½ stick (¼ cup) butter or
  margarine

················ **FOR 8-INCH SQUARE CAKE** ·················
·········· **(OR BARS OR GLAZING BUNDT CAKES*)** ··········

3-ounce package cream   ¾ cup powdered sugar
  cheese   1 teaspoon vanilla
2 tablespoons butter or
  margarine

1. Microwave cream cheese, unwrapped, and butter in a microwave-safe mixing bowl for 45 to 60 seconds at MEDIUM HIGH (70%), or until softened but not melted. Add remaining ingredients and beat until fluffy.

Yield: Frosting for 1 9 × 13-inch or 8-inch square cake.

———————— · ❄ · ————————

OLD-FASHIONED PENUCHE FROSTING MADE EASY

½ stick (¼ cup) butter or   2 tablespoons milk
  margarine   1 cup powdered sugar
½ cup brown sugar,
  packed

···
*Bundt Cake Glaze: Microwave beaten frosting for 30 seconds at HIGH (100%). Immediately drizzle over bundt cake.

To be more economical, you can use only 3 ounces cream cheese in the 9×13-inch recipe. No other adjustment is necessary.

You can add 1 to 3 teaspoons of milk to thin this traditional frosting, if desired.

1. Microwave butter in a 1-quart microwave-safe bowl for 30 seconds at HIGH (100%). Stir in brown sugar and microwave again for 2 minutes at HIGH (100%).
2. Stir in milk. Microwave for 1 minute at HIGH (100%). Cool until lukewarm.
3. Beat in powdered sugar, stirring until thick.

Yield: Frosting for 1-layer cake or 12 cupcakes.

———————— · ❄ · ————————

TIPS
....

Carob powder is the perfect caffeine-free substitute for cocoa. See the tip on page 48 for additional information on using carob.

CAROB FROSTING

———————— · · · · · ————————

Chocolate free, but tastes like chocolate!

3 tablespoons butter or margarine
3 tablespoons carob powder

1½ cups powdered sugar
2 tablespoons milk
½ teaspoon vanilla

1. Microwave butter in a 1-quart microwave-safe bowl for 20 to 30 seconds at HIGH (100%) to melt. Stir in carob powder. Beat in powdered sugar, milk, and vanilla until smooth. Spread on slightly cooled bars or cake.

Yield: Frosting for 1 8-inch cake or pan of bars.

———————— · ❄ · ————————

CHOCOLATE CHIPPER FROSTING

• • • • •

Easy and tasty frosting for brownies or cake.

TIPS

Use this recipe any time you need a quick and delicious frosting for brownies, bars, or cakes. It also works well drizzled on bundt cakes.

············· **FOR 9 × 13-INCH CAKE OR BARS** ·············

1½ cups sugar
⅓ cup butter or margarine

⅓ cup milk
1 cup (6 ounces) semisweet
   chocolate chips

·········· **FOR 8-INCH SQUARE CAKE OR BARS** ··········

¾ cup sugar
2½ tablespoons butter or
   margarine

2½ tablespoons milk
½ cup (3 ounces) chocolate
   chips

1. In a 1-quart microwave-safe bowl, combine sugar, butter, and milk. Microwave for 2 to 3 minutes at HIGH (100%), until mixture boils.
2. Stir in chocolate chips until smooth. Frost cake or brownies immediately.

Yield: Frosting for 1 9 × 13-inch or 8-inch square cake.

FAST FUDGE FROSTING

• • • • •

½ cup sugar
2 tablespoons
   unsweetened cocoa
2 tablespoons butter or
   margarine
4 tablespoons milk

1 tablespoon light corn
   syrup
Dash of salt
⅔ cup powdered sugar
½ teaspoon vanilla

1. Combine sugar and cocoa in a 2-quart microwave-safe bowl. Add butter, milk, corn syrup, and salt. Microwave

for 2 to 3 minutes at MEDIUM HIGH (70%), until boiling. Stir. Continue to microwave for 2½ to 3 minutes longer at MEDIUM HIGH (70%). Cool.
2. Beat in powdered sugar and vanilla.

Yield: Frosting for 1 8-inch cake or pan of bars.

——————— · ❋ · ———————

TIPS
········

I like to use this frosting with pudding-in-the-mix German chocolate, chocolate, or butter brickle cake batter.

The Tropical Fruit Frosting is delicious with yellow pudding-in-the-mix cake batters.

COCONUT PECAN FROSTING
—————— · · · · · ——————

A self-frosting for any cake: frost and cook the cake at once!

⅓ cup butter or margarine
⅔ cup brown sugar, packed
¾ cup (3 ounces) chopped pecans or walnuts

½ cup shredded coconut
¼ cup evaporated milk or half-and-half

1. Microwave butter and brown sugar in a microwave bundt pan for 1 to 2 minutes at HIGH (100%), until bubbly. Sprinkle with pecans and coconut. Pour milk over coconut.
2. Microwave again for 1 to 1½ minutes at HIGH (100%), until bubbly. Stir and spread evenly in pan.
3. Pour any mixed cake batter (mixed according to package directions) over the hot topping and microwave.
(For any pudding-in-the-mix cake batter: Microwave for 11 minutes at DEFROST [30%] and for 6 to 7 minutes at HIGH [100%]. Let stand 15 minutes. Invert.)

Yield: Self-frosting for 1 bundt cake.

—————— · ❋ · ——————

Variation: Tropical Fruit Frosting: Substitute ½ cup crushed pineapple for the ¼ cup evaporated milk. Add ¼ cup chopped maraschino cherries with the pineapple (optional).

HOLIDAY SAUCES AND ICE CREAMS

· ❄ ·

LEMON SAUCE

· · · · ·

½ stick (¼ cup) butter or
   margarine
⅔ cup sugar
1½ tablespoons cornstarch

¾ cup water
2 tablespoons lemon juice
½ teaspoon grated lemon
   peel (zest only)

1. Microwave butter for 20 to 30 seconds at HIGH (100%) in a 1-quart microwave-safe bowl. Combine sugar and cornstarch. Add to butter. Stir in water, lemon juice, and peel.
2. Microwave for 2 to 3 minutes at HIGH (100%), until boiling, stirring once. Serve warm, if desired, over bread puddings, cake, ice cream, fruit cups, and so on.

Yield: 1 cup sauce.

· ❄ ·

Try Quick Fudge Sauce in an ice cream pie: Fill a 9-inch chocolate cookie pie crust with 1 quart vanilla ice cream. Drizzle Quick Fudge Sauce on top and decorate with pecans. Freeze until serving time.

To reheat Quick Fudge Sauce: Microwave one-fourth cup for 20 to 30 seconds at HIGH (100%). Drizzle over ice cream or cake.

To reheat chilled sauce: Microwave 2 tablespoons in a custard cup for 10 to 15 seconds at HIGH (100%).

QUICK FUDGE SAUCE

3 tablespoons butter or margarine
½ cup milk
1 cup (6 ounces) semisweet chocolate chips

1 cup miniature or 11 large marshmallows
Dash of salt

1. Combine all ingredients in a 1-quart microwave-safe bowl. Microwave for 3 to 4 minutes at HIGH (100%), stirring occasionally until marshmallows look very soft and puffy. Stir until smooth. Cool slightly and serve warm, if desired.

Yield: 1 cup sauce.

HOT CHOCOLATE FUDGE SAUCE

3 tablespoons butter or margarine
1 cup sugar
¼ cup unsweetened cocoa
Dash salt

1 tablespoon flour
2 tablespoons light corn syrup
⅓ cup milk
1 teaspoon vanilla

1. Microwave butter in a 1-quart microwave-safe bowl for 25 to 30 seconds at HIGH (100%) or until melted.
2. Combine dry ingredients and stir into melted butter. Stir in remaining ingredients, except vanilla.
3. Microwave uncovered for 2½ to 4 minutes at HIGH (100%) or until boiling. Stir in vanilla. Serve warm over ice cream or cake. Refrigerate remainder and use as needed.

Yield: 1 cup sauce.

PRALINE SAUCE

A taste sensation over ice cream or cooked fruit.

½ cup light corn syrup
½ cup brown sugar,
   packed
½ stick (¼ cup) butter or
   margarine, softened

½ cup (2 ounces) pecans,
   halves or chopped
   pieces
1 teaspoon vanilla

1. Combine corn syrup, brown sugar, and butter in a 1-quart microwave-safe bowl. Microwave for 2 minutes at HIGH (100%), or until mixture boils.
2. Stir and microwave again for 30 seconds at HIGH (100%) while boiling.
3. Stir in pecans and vanilla. Delicious! Serve warm over ice cream, custard, or cooked fruit.

Yield: 1½ cups sauce.

BANANA SPLIT ROYAL SAUCE

1 cup Quick Fudge or 1½
   cups Praline Sauce or 12
   ounces of your favorite
   ice cream topping
1 cup miniature
   marshmallows or 12
   large ones

2 bananas, sliced
½ cup (2 ounces) walnuts,
   almonds, or pecans
   (omit if using Praline
   Sauce)
½ cup maraschino cherries

TIPS

For Quick Fudge or Praline Sauce, see page 157 or above.

1. Combine all ingredients in a microwave-safe 2-quart bowl (or plastic cooking bag tied and placed in a bowl for easy cleanup).

2. Microwave for 3 to 4 minutes at MEDIUM HIGH (70%),* until heated. Spoon over ice cream.

Yield: 4 to 6 servings.

———————— · ❄ · ————————

TIPS
········

Use either fresh or frozen blueberries. If you use frozen blue-berries, thaw slightly by microwaving for 1 to 1½ minutes at HIGH (100%) before adding to the cornstarch mix-ture in step #1.

EASY BLUEBERRY SAUCE
———— · · · · · ————

Great over cheese cake, pound cake, or ice cream!

2 tablespoons cornstarch   ¾ cup sugar
2 teaspoons lemon juice   2 cups blueberries
¼ cup water

1. Combine all ingredients, except blueberries, in a 1-quart microwave-safe bowl. Mix until smooth. Then stir in the blueberries.
2. Microwave for 2 minutes at HIGH (100%). Mix well and continue microwaving for 1 to 2 minutes at HIGH (100%), or until thickened (175°F.). Cool. (Sauce will thicken further when chilled.)

Yield: 1½ to 2 cups sauce.

———————— · ❄ · ————————

STRAWBERRY OR RASPBERRY SAUCE
———— · · · · · ————

10-ounce package frozen   1 tablespoon cornstarch
   strawberries or   1 drop red food coloring
   raspberries   (optional)

··

*Compacts: Microwave for 3 to 3½ minutes at HIGH (100%) in step #2.

1. Thaw strawberries by microwaving in a microwave-safe bowl for 1½ to 3½ minutes at HIGH (100%). Drain, reserving juice.
2. Combine cornstarch and reserved juice in a 1-quart microwave-safe bowl. Stir in strawberries. Microwave for 3 to 4 minutes at HIGH (100%), until thickened and clear, stirring twice. Add food coloring, if desired.

Yield: 1 cup sauce.

———————— · ❄ · ————————

C I N N A M O N S A U C E

———————— · · · · · ————————

Great on apple pie and ice cream!

¾ cup sugar
⅓ cup light corn syrup

3 tablespoons butter or margarine
1½ teaspoons cinnamon

1. Combine all ingredients in a 2-quart microwave-safe bowl. Microwave for 2 minutes at HIGH (100%). Stir.
2. Microwave for 1 to 2 minutes at HIGH (100%), or until boiling. Serve warm.

Yield: 1 cup sauce.

———————— · ❄ · ————————

T I P S
....

In a pinch for a fast dessert to top off a special meal or evening? Bake a frozen apple pie as the package directs. Serve warm slices of pie topped with ice cream and warm Cinnamon Sauce!

Try one of the new nonelectric models of ice cream freezers that require no salt and no ice. The outer compartment is chilled in the freezer before adding the custard mixture. Once the custard mixture is added, the ice cream is ready in approximately 20 minutes.

OLD-FASHIONED CHOCOLATE CUSTARD ICE CREAM

1½ cups sugar
½ cup unsweetened cocoa
1 tablespoon cornstarch
⅛ teaspoon salt

1½ cups milk
2 large eggs, beaten
1 tablespoon vanilla
2 cups whipping cream

1. Combine sugar, cocoa, cornstarch, and salt in a 2-quart microwave-safe bowl. Gradually stir in milk. Microwave for 5 to 6 minutes at HIGH (100%), until boiling, stirring twice. Add a small amount of this milk mixture to the beaten eggs and mix quickly. Beat eggs into milk mixture.
2. Microwave again for 1 to 2 minutes at MEDIUM (50%) to thicken. Cool completely. Stir in vanilla and cream. Freeze using an ice cream freezer as directed by manufacturer.

Yield: 2 quarts ice cream.

FRENCH VANILLA ICE CREAM

Smooth and creamy (with strawberry variation)

⅔ cup sugar
2 cups milk
⅛ teaspoon salt

4 large egg yolks, beaten
1 tablespoon vanilla
2 cups whipping cream

1. Combine sugar, milk, and salt in a 2-quart microwave-safe bowl. Microwave for 3 to 4 minutes at HIGH (100%), until very hot. Add a small amount of the hot milk to the beaten egg yolks and mix quickly. Beat egg yolks into milk and sugar.

2. Microwave for 6 minutes at MEDIUM (50%). Stir well. Microwave again for 4 to 5 minutes at MEDIUM (50%), until mixture boils. Beat lightly. Cool completely. Stir in vanilla and cream. Freeze using an ice cream freezer as directed by manufacturer.

Yield: 2 quarts ice cream.

———————— · ❄ · ————————

Variation: Strawberry Ice Cream: Omit vanilla. Add 1 pint prepared and crushed fresh strawberries or 10 ounces frozen strawberries, thawed slightly and crushed with the cream in step #2.

Variation: Vanilla Ice Cream: Substitute 2 eggs for the 4 yolks and substitute 2 cups half-and-half for the whipping cream. Proceed as directed.

LITE VANILLA ICE CREAM

Low-fat (with peppermint variation).

2 12-ounce cans
  evaporated skim milk
1 envelope unflavored
  gelatin

¾ cup sugar
2 tablespoons vanilla
1 cup low-fat plain or
  vanilla yogurt

1. Combine milk and gelatin in a 2-quart microwave-safe bowl. Microwave for 5 to 6 minutes at MEDIUM HIGH (70%), stirring twice, until gelatin is dissolved. Stir in sugar until blended and dissolved. Whisk or whip in vanilla and yogurt until well blended.
2. Freeze using an ice cream freezer as directed by manufacturer. Or freeze 1 hour in a 9 × 13-inch metal pan, then beat with an electric mixer until smooth. Repeat procedure one more time, then freeze solid.

Yield: 2 quarts ice cream.

———————— · ❄ · ————————

Variation: Peppermint Ice Cream: Reduce vanilla to 1 teaspoon. Add ½ teaspoon peppermint extract. After freezing in the ice cream freezer, fold in ¾ cup crushed peppermint candies.

CHOCOLATE - PECAN ICE CREAM CUPS

——————— · · · · · ———————

14-ounce can sweetened
   condensed milk
2 cups (12 ounces)
   semisweet chocolate
   chips

1 cup (4 ounces) finely
   chopped pecans
1 teaspoon burnt sugar
   flavoring or almond
   extract

1. Microwave condensed milk and chocolate chips in a 2-quart microwave-safe bowl for 3 to 4½ minutes at MEDIUM HIGH (70%), or until chips start to melt. Stir until smooth. Blend in finely chopped pecans and flavoring.
2. Line 16 2½-inch muffin cups with foil liners. Spoon 1 heaping tablespoon of the mixture into each liner. Using a teaspoon, thoroughly coat the bottoms and sides of each liner with the chocolate mixture. Freeze at least 2 hours before serving. At serving time, remove foil liners and fill with your favorite ice cream.

Yield: 16 cups.

 ——————— · ❆ · ———————

HOLIDAY PIES

❄

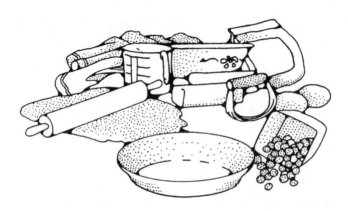

*THANKSGIVING AND CHRISTMAS SEASON
PIES*

NESSELROAD PIE

An old-fashioned delicacy made a new-fashioned way!

1 envelope unflavored
  gelatin
⅓ cup sugar
2 teaspoons cornstarch
2 large egg yolks, beaten
⅔ cup milk
2 tablespoons maraschino
  cherry syrup
8 ounces (3½ cups)
  whipped topping

⅓ cup maraschino
  cherries, cut in fourths
¾ cup (3 ounces) chopped
  almonds, toasted
9-inch vanilla wafer or
  graham cracker crust
  (see page 187)
24 green gumdrops to
  garnish, optional

(see page 187)

TIPS

To toast almonds: Micro-
wave ¾ cup slivered
almonds with 1 tea-
spoon butter on a paper
plate for 3 to 4 minutes
at HIGH (100%), until
browned and crisp, stir-
ring twice. Chop.

To make holly leaves:
Roll gumdrops ⅛-inch
thick on a sugared sur-
face. Cut into leaf
shapes.

1. Combine gelatin, sugar, and cornstarch in a 2-quart microwave-safe bowl. Stir in egg yolks and milk, blending until smooth. Microwave for 3½ to 4 minutes at HIGH (100%), until mixture boils, stirring twice. Stir in maraschino cherry syrup.
2. Refrigerate 30 minutes until mixture mounds slightly.
3. Fold in 2 cups of the whipped topping, the cherries, and the toasted almonds. Pour into prepared crust. Refrigerate until serving time. Serve garnished with the remaining whipped topping with additional cherries and holly leaves made from gumdrops (see tip).

Yield: 1 9-inch pie.

———————— · ❄ · ————————

TIPS
....

For an even easier holiday dessert, start with a prepared chocolate pie crust from the baking section of your grocery store.

CHOCOLATE FUDGE AND MINT PIE

———————— · · · · · ————————

A quick and lovely dessert—great for the Christmas season!

·························· **FILLING** ··························

1 quart mint ice cream (green)	9-inch chocolate cookie crust (See page 187)

·············· **CHOCOLATE FUDGE SAUCE** ··············

1 tablespoon butter or margarine	½ cup miniature or 12 large marshmallows
¼ cup milk	Dash of salt
½ cup semisweet chocolate chips	Whipping topping and peppermint candy, to garnish (optional)

1. **Filling:** Soften ice cream by microwaving 1-quart for 1 to 1½ minutes at DEFROST (30%). Spread into prepared chocolate cookie crust. Freeze.
2. Combine all chocolate fudge sauce ingredients in a 1-quart microwave-safe bowl. Microwave for 2 to 3 minutes at HIGH (100%), stirring occasionally, until marshmallows look very soft and puffy. Stir until smooth. Cool to room temperature.
3. Drizzle chocolate sauce over prepared crust and ice cream. Freeze. (Cover with aluminum foil if prepared more than a few hours in advance of serving.)
4. Serve garnished with a dollop of whipped topping and a peppermint candy piece or broken candy cane.

Yield: 1 9-inch pie.

———————— · ❄ · ————————

COCONUT PECAN PIE
——————— · · · · · ———————

A holiday perfect pie that's too good to be true!

(Use your convection microwave or your conventional oven and your microwave as a team.)

¾ cup brown sugar, packed

¾ cup sugar

½ cup milk

¾ cup rolled oats (quick or regular)

¾ cup shredded coconut

½ stick (¼ cup) butter or margarine, softened

3 medium eggs, well beaten

2 teaspoons vanilla

¾ cup (3 ounces) broken pecan halves

9-inch pie shell (unbaked) in a glass or microwave-safe pie plate

. . . .

The secret of happy living is not to do what you like, but to like what you do.

TIPS
. . . .

Three convection microwave settings are suggested. Choose the one that corresponds to the power setting on your microwave.

If you don't own a convection microwave, try this recipe using both your conventional oven and your microwave. It works equally well.

1. Combine all ingredients except pie shell in a 2-quart mixing bowl, adding pecans last. Pour into the pie shell.
2. **For convection microwave:** Preheat oven to 400°F. Low-Mix Bake on a raised rack at 400° for 22 to 25 minutes, or until set (or use Combination 2 or Code 2 for 30 minutes).

   For microwave and a regular oven: Preheat your regular (conventional) oven to 400°F. Bake for 20 minutes; then microwave for 5 minutes at MEDIUM HIGH (70%), or until set.

Yield: 1 9-inch pie.

———————— · ❄ · ————————

TIPS
········

This pie will serve eight to ten people because you can cut the pieces small. It's so rich that a sliver is all that is needed.

CHOCOLATE PEANUT BUTTER PIE

———————— · · · · · ————————

3-ounce package cream cheese
¾ cup powdered sugar
½ cup creamy or crunchy peanut butter
8 ounces (3½ cups) whipped topping

9-inch chocolate cookie crust (see page 187)
½ cup (3 ounces) milk chocolate chips
1 tablespoon milk
2 tablespoons butter or margarine

1. Microwave cream cheese, unwrapped, in a 2-quart microwave-safe bowl for 30 to 40 seconds at MEDIUM HIGH (70%) to soften. Stir in powdered sugar and peanut butter. Fold in whipped topping. Pour into chocolate cookie crust.
2. Microwave chocolate chips, milk, and butter in a 1-quart microwave-safe bowl for 1 to 1½ minutes at MEDIUM HIGH (70%), or until chips start to melt. Stir until smooth. Spread over cream cheese filling. Refrigerate until serving time.

Yield: 1 9-inch pie.

———————— · ❄ · ————————

BLACK CADILLAC PIE
(OR GRASSHOPPER PIE VARIATION)

— • • • • • —

A delightful after-dinner pie!

4 cups miniature
  marshmallows (or 44
  large)
½ cup milk
⅓ cup Irish creme or
  crème de cocoa
1 cup (6 ounces) semisweet
  chocolate chips,
  chopped

1 cup (8 ounces) whipping
  cream, whipped
9-inch chocolate cookie
  crust (see page 187)
Additional whipped cream
  or whipped topping and
  chocolate curls to
  garnish, optional

1. Microwave marshmallows and milk in a 2-quart microwave-safe bowl for 2 to 2½ minutes at HIGH (100%),
   stirring twice. Stir until smooth. Stir in Irish creme. Refrigerate until thickened, approximately 45 minutes. Stir
   in chocolate chips.
2. Fold whipped cream into marshmallow mixture. Pour
   into prepared crust. Freeze or refrigerate until set. (If
   frozen, transfer to refrigerator ½ hour before serving.)
   Serve garnished with whipped topping and chocolate curls
   or a chocolate dinner mint, if desired.

Yield: 1 9-inch pie.

———— • ❉ • ————

Variation: Grasshopper Pie: Substitute 3 tablespoons
green crème de menthe and 2 tablespoons crème de cocoa for
the ⅓ cup Irish creme. Omit chocolate chips. Add 3 drops
green food coloring (optional). Proceed as directed.

TIPS
....

You can substitute a
graham cracker crust
for the chocolate cookie
crust, if desired.

To chop chocolate
chips, process in a food
processor or blender
until coarsely chopped.

You can substitute 1
cup (6 ounces) minia-
ture chocolate chips for
the chopped chocolate
chips.

FAST-MIX PUMPKIN PIE

Either filling will produce a quick and delicious pie.

You can substitute 1 teaspoon cinnamon, ½ teaspoon nutmeg, ¼ teaspoon ginger, and ⅛ teaspoon allspice for 2 teaspoons pumpkin pie spice in the traditional filling.

·············· PUMPKIN PIE MIX FILLING ················

30-ounce can pumpkin pie
    mix

5⅓ ounce can evaporated
    milk (⅔ cup)
2 large eggs, beaten

·················· TRADITIONAL FILLING ··················

16-ounce can pumpkin
14-ounce can sweetened
    condensed milk (not
    evaporated)

2 large eggs, beaten
2 teaspoons pumpkin pie
    spice

················· OLD-FASHIONED FILLING ··················

16-ounce can pumpkin
2 large eggs
2 tablespoons flour
1 cup brown sugar,
    packed

2 teaspoons pumpkin pie
    spice
1¼ cups evaporated or
    whole milk

························· CRUST ·························

9-inch baked pie shell (in a
    glass or microwave-safe
    pie plate)

1. Combine all the ingredients for filling of your choice in a 2-quart microwave-safe bowl. Using an electric mixer, beat until smooth. Cover with plastic wrap (vent on edge). Microwave for 8 minutes at MEDIUM (50%), stirring twice.
2. Pour filling into baked pie crust. Place on an inverted pie plate in oven. Microwave for 22 to 25 minutes at MEDIUM (50%), until center is almost set but looks

slightly moist rotating pie once halfway through cooking time. Let stand 10 minutes.

Yield: 1 9-inch pie.

———————— · ❄ · ————————

For Convection-Microwave: Start with an unbaked crust. Proceed as directed in step #1. Convection microwave at Low Mix Bake 350° (or Combination #2 or Code #2) for 25 to 30 minutes. Let stand 10 minutes.

COCONUT CREAM PIE IN A CHOCOLATE COCONUT CRUST

————— · · · · · —————

TIPS
········

The crust and filling for this delicious pie can easily be prepared in the microwave oven, but use the conventional oven for the meringue, when possible.

I prefer the traditional texture and browned meringue baked in a conventional oven. The microwave produces a light and firm meringue with a somewhat spongey texture.

For a broiled meringue, see tip (Lemon Merinque Pie) on page 175.

·················· CRUST ··························

1/ 2 cup semisweet
   chocolate chips

3 tablespoons butter or
   margarine
2 cups shredded coconut

·················· FILLING ·······················

⅔ cup sugar
¼ cup cornstarch
1½ cups milk
3 large eggs

¾ cup shredded coconut
1 teaspoon vanilla
2 tablespoons butter or
   margarine

················ MERINGUE TOPPING ··················

3 egg whites

½ teaspoon cream of tartar
⅓ cup sugar

1. **Crust:** Microwave chocolate chips and butter in a 1-quart microwave-safe bowl for 1 to 1½ minutes at MEDIUM HIGH (70%). Stir until melted. Stir in coconut.

2. Microwave for 1 to 2 minutes at HIGH (100%), until bubbly. Stir. Cool 10 minutes. Press all but ⅓ cup of the coconut mixture into a 9-inch pie plate to form crust.

3. **Filling:** Combine sugar and cornstarch in a 1-quart microwave-safe bowl. Add milk; blend until smooth. Microwave for 4 minutes at HIGH (100%), until thickened. Stir.

4. In a small bowl, beat eggs and add ¼ cup of the hot milk mixture, stirring constantly. Stir egg mixture quickly into hot milk. Microwave for 1½ to 2 minutes at MEDIUM HIGH (70%), until mixture bubbles around the edges. Stir in coconut, vanilla, and butter. Carefully pour into chocolate coconut crust.

5. **Meringue Topping:** Beat egg whites with cream of tartar until stiff peaks form. Gradually beat in sugar until whites become glossy. Spread over hot pie, sealing edges well.

   For a browned crust: Bake in conventional oven (preheated) at 400° for 9 to 10 minutes.

   Or for a firm but *not* brown crust: Microwave 2½ to 3½ minutes at MEDIUM (50%) or until meringue is set.

6. Sprinkle with reserved chocolate-coconut to garnish. Cool.

Yield: 1 9-inch pie.

————— · ❄ · —————

Variation: Traditional Coconut Cream Pie: Substitute a baked pie shell or graham cracker crust for the chocolate coconut crust. Omit steps #1 and # 2. Garnish with toasted coconut. (See page 188.)

EGGNOG PIE

. . . . .

1 envelope unflavored
　gelatin
1¼ cups milk
¾ cup sugar, divided
3 medium eggs, separated
Dash of salt
½ teaspoon nutmeg
1 teaspoon vanilla
1 teaspoon rum flavoring

2 cups (4½ ounces)
　whipped topping or
　whipped cream
9-inch vanilla wafer or
　graham cracker crust or
　baked pastry crust (see
　pages 187, 189)
Maraschino cherries to
　garnish, optional

1. Combine gelatin and milk; set aside. Beat ½ cup sugar, 3
   egg yolks, and salt in a 2-quart microwave-safe bowl until
   foamy. Beat in gelatin and milk. Microwave for 3 to 4
   minutes at MEDIUM HIGH (70%), or until boiling,
   stirring twice. Stir in nutmeg, vanilla, and rum flavoring.
   Cool until thickened but not set.
2. Beat egg whites until frothy. Gradually add remaining ¼
   cup sugar; beat until stiff.
3. Gently fold whipped topping and then beaten egg whites
   into gelatin mixture.
4. Fold into prepared crust. Chill until firm (4 hours). Serve
   each slice garnished with additional whipped topping and
   a cherry.

Yield: 1 9-inch pie.

———————— · ❄ · ————————

MOTHER'S DAY, VICTORIA DAY, AND SPRINGTIME PIES

TIPS
....

This recipe is the micro-wave version of a rec-ipe I brought back from our honeymoon in Orlando, Florida.

The pie will look set around the edges but will still jiggle after mi-crowaving. It will set up further when cooled.

QUICK KEY LIME PIE

· · · · ·

14-ounce can sweetened
  condensed milk
½ cup lime juice
2 to 3 drops green food
  coloring (optional)

3 large eggs, separated
10-inch graham cracker
  crust (see page 187)
8 ounces (3½ cups)
  whipped topping

1. Combine milk, lime juice, food coloring, and beaten egg yolks. Beat egg whites until stiff; fold into milk mixture. Pour into pie crust.
2. Microwave 6 to 8 minutes at DEFROST (30%). Cool. Refrigerate until serving. Top with whipped topping, and sprinkle with grated lime peel before serving, if desired.

Yield: 1 10-inch pie.

———— · ❄ · ————

This pineapple pie freezes well. If frozen, transfer to the re-frigerator half an hour before serving.

COOL AND SWEET PINEAPPLE PIE

· · · · ·

¾ cup sugar, divided
8-ounce can crushed
  pineapple, drained (save
  juice or syrup)
2 teaspoons lemon juice
3 large eggs, separated

3-ounce package lemon
  gelatin, dry
1 cup (2 ounces) whipped
  topping
9-inch graham cracker or
  vanilla wafer crust (see
  page 187)

1. Combine ½ cup sugar, reserved pineapple juice, and lemon juice in a 2-quart microwave-safe bowl. Stir beaten egg yolks into juices. Mix well. Microwave for 3 to 4

minutes at HIGH (100%), or until mixture thickens slightly, stirring twice.

2. Stir in lemon gelatin until dissolved. Stir in pineapple. Cool.
3. Beat egg whites until stiff; beat in ¼ cup sugar. Fold in cooled pineapple mixture and whipped topping.
4. Pour into the graham cracker crust. Refrigerate at least 4 hours or freeze, if desired. Serve garnished with additional whipped topping and maraschino cherries.

Yield: 1 9-inch pie.

———————— · ❄ · ————————

CHOCOLATE CHIFFON PIE

————————— · · · · · —————————

1 envelope unflavored
  gelatin
½ cup cold water
2 ounces (2 squares)
  unsweetened chocolate
½ cup hot water

4 medium eggs, separated
1 teaspoon vanilla
1 cup sugar
9-inch graham cracker
  crust (see page 187)

.... GARNISH ....

1 cup (2 ounces) whipped
  topping

½ square chocolate bar,
  shaved (2 ounces)

1. **Pie:** In a 2-quart microwave-safe bowl, dissolve gelatin in cold water. Add chocolate and hot water. Microwave for 2 to 3 minutes at HIGH (100%), until chocolate looks softened and can be stirred smooth.
2. Add well-beaten egg yolks, vanilla, and ½ cup sugar. Mix well. Microwave at HIGH (100%) for 2 minutes. Stir. Cool until mixture mounds when spooned.
3. Beat egg whites until stiff, adding ½ cup sugar.
4. Gently fold whites into cooled chocolate mixture.

5. Spoon into crust. Refrigerate until firm (about 4 hours).
6. **Garnish:** Garnish with whipped topping and shaved chocolate.

Yield: 1 9-inch pie.

· ❄ ·

LEMON MERINGUE PIE

· · · · ·

·········· FILLING ··········

1½ cups sugar
⅓ cup plus 1 tablespoon cornstarch
1½ cups water
Dash of salt
3 large eggs, separated

3 teaspoons finely grated lemon peel (zest only)
3 tablespoons butter or margarine
½ cup lemon juice
9-inch baked pie crust (see pages 188–189)

·········· MERINGUE ··········

Egg whites from eggs in filling
½ teaspoon cream of tartar

⅓ cup sugar
½ teaspoon vanilla

1. **Filling:** Combine sugar, cornstarch, salt, and water in a 2-quart microwave-safe bowl. Slowly stir in water until completely blended and cornstarch is dissolved. Microwave for 7½ to 9 minutes at MEDIUM HIGH (70%), until thickened, stirring three to four times.
2. Beat egg yolks in a small bowl. Stir into yolks 3 tablespoons of the cooked mixture until blended, then add the yolks to the cooked mixture. Microwave for 1½ to 3 minutes at MEDIUM HIGH (70%).* Stir in lemon peel, butter, and lemon juice. Pour into prepared crust.

···
*Compacts: Microwave at HIGH (100%) for the amount of time directed.

TIPS
·······

See tip for grating lemon zest (for Lemon Bars Deluxe) on page 39.

I prefer the traditional texture and browned meringue baked in a conventional oven. The microwave produces a light and firm meringue with a spongey texture.

You can also brown meringue under the broiler. Microwave meringue on pie for 1 minute at MEDIUM (50%) and broil for 1 minute, or until lightly browned.

3. **Meringue:** Beat egg whites with cream of tartar until stiff peaks form. Gradually beat in sugar until whites become glossy. Stir in vanilla. Spread over hot pie, sealing edges well. Bake or microwave as directed below. Cool before serving.

For a browned crust: Bake in your conventional oven (preheated) at 400°F. for 9 to 10 minutes until lightly browned.

Or for a firm but unbrowned crust: Microwave 2½ to 3½ minutes at MEDIUM (50%), or until meringue is set.

Yield: 9-inch pie.

· ❄ ·

LEMONADE PIE

· · · · ·

It tastes as good and sweet as it sounds!

···················· FILLING ····························

½ cup sugar
¼ cup cornstarch
6-ounce can frozen
    lemonade concentrate
4 medium eggs, separated

1 tablespoon butter or
    margarine
1 cup hot water
9-inch pretzel crust (see
    page 187)

···················· MERINGUE ························

Egg whites from eggs in
    filling

½ cup sugar

1. **Filling:** Combine ½ cup sugar and cornstarch in a small bowl. Set aside. Microwave opened can of lemonade for 30 to 40 seconds at HIGH (100%) to thaw. Stir

TIPS
········

Microwave the lemonade in the can to thaw it. Simply remove the top lid first and proceed as directed in step #1.

The small amount of metal on the bottom of the can can be used in most microwave ovens without harming the oven. Check your manufacturer's instruction book to make sure.

lemonade and beaten egg yolks into cornstarch and sugar. Set aside.

2. In a 2-quart microwave-safe bowl, combine butter and hot water, stirring until butter melts. Slowly add lemonade mixture, stirring well. Microwave for 4½ to 6 minutes at MEDIUM HIGH (70%),* until thickened (180°F.). Cool.

3. **Meringue:** In a cool, dry bowl with clean beaters, beat egg whites until frothy. Add ½ cup sugar and beat until stiff.

4. Fold about one-third of the meringue into the slightly cooled lemonade filling. Pour the filling into the prepared crust.

5. Top filling with the remaining meringue, spreading to seal edges. Bake or microwave as directed below.

For a browned crust: Bake in your conventional oven (preheated) at 400°F. for 9 to 10 minutes until lightly browned.

For a firm but unbrowned crust: Microwave 2½ to 3½ minutes at MEDIUM (50%), or until meringue is set.

Yield: 1 9-inch pie.

———————— · ❄ · ————————

---

*Compacts: Microwave at HIGH (100%) for the same amount of time directed.

BANANA CREAM PIE

A microwave recipe converted from a state fair winner!

.... FILLING ....

⅔ cup sugar

⅓ cup cornstarch

½ teaspoon salt

2¼ cups milk

3 large eggs, separated

2 teaspoons vanilla

½ stick (¼ cup) butter

3 large, firm bananas

9-inch baked pie crust or vanilla wafer crust (see pages 188–189, 187)

.... MERINGUE ....

Egg whites (from filling)

½ teaspoon cream of tartar

⅓ cup sugar

½ teaspoon vanilla

1. **Filling:** Combine sugar, cornstarch, and salt in a 2-quart microwave-safe bowl. Slowly stir in milk until completely blended. Add beaten egg yolks and beat well. Microwave for 7½ to 9 minutes at MEDIUM HIGH (70%), until mixture boils, stirring twice. Stir in vanilla and butter. Set aside.

2. Slice bananas and gently fold into the filling. Pour into prepared crust. Set aside.

3. **Meringue:** Beat egg whites with cream of tartar until stiff peaks form. Gradually beat in sugar until glossy. Stir in vanilla. Spread over pie filling, sealing edges well. Bake or microwave as directed below. Cool before serving.

Or for a browned crust: Bake in your conventional oven (preheated) 400°F. for 9 to 10 minutes until lightly browned.

For a firm but unbrowned crust: Microwave for 2½ to 3½ minutes at MEDIUM (50%), or until meringue is set.

Yield: 1 9-inch pie.

———— · ❄ · ————

For additional tips on cooking the meringue, see tips on page 175 for Lemon Meringue Pie.

You can substitute 8 ounces whipped topping or 2 cups whipped cream (1 cup before whipping) for the meringue. Omit step #3 and spread topping on cooled pie.

TIPS

Independence Day Pie is the perfect dessert for any patriotic celebration. It is simply a cheese cake filling sandwiched between blueberries and strawberries.

For a quick pie, substitute one 20-ounce can blueberry pie filling for the blue layer and one 20-ounce can of strawberry pie filling for the red layer. Use a store-bought graham cracker crust. Proceed as directed for the white layer.

INDEPENDENCE DAY PIE

· · · · ·

·············· BLUE LAYER ··············

2 cups fresh or frozen
   blueberries, divided
⅓ cup water

¼ cup sugar
1 tablespoon cornstarch
9-inch graham cracker
   crust (see page 187)

·············· WHITE LAYER ··············

8-ounce package cream
   cheese
½ cup sugar

1 teaspoon vanilla
1 medium egg

·············· RED LAYER ··············

3 cups freshly prepared
   strawberries
½ cup sugar

¼ cup water
2 tablespoons cornstarch

·············· GARNISH ··············

1 cup whipped cream or
   whipped topping plus
   extra berries (optional)

1. **Blue layer:** Combine 1 cup blueberries, water, sugar, and cornstarch in a 1-quart microwave-safe bowl. Microwave for 2 to 3 minutes at HIGH (100%), until boiling, stirring twice. Cool. Stir in remaining blueberries. Pour into prepared crust.
2. **White layer:** Microwave cream cheese, unwrapped, in a 1-quart microwave-safe bowl for 30 to 40 seconds at

MEDIUM HIGH (70%) to soften. Stir in sugar, vanilla, and egg. Microwave for 3 to 4 minutes at MEDIUM HIGH (70%), until thickened. Pour over cooled blueberry (blue) layer in the pie crust.

3. **Red layer:** Mash 1 cup of strawberries in a 1-quart microwave-safe bowl; refrigerate remainder. Add sugar and 2 tablespoons water to the mashed berries. Microwave for 2 to 3 minutes at HIGH (100%), until boiling. Mix cornstarch and 2 tablespoons water. Add to boiling mixture. Microwave for 2 minutes at HIGH (100%), until thickened. Cool. Fold in strawberries. Spread on top of white layer. Refrigerate at least 2 to 3 hours. Serve garnished with a dollop of whipped cream, additional blueberries, and large whole strawberries, if desired.

Yield: 1 9-inch pie.

· ❄ · ─────

CANADA DAY SASKATOON PIE

····

(Use your convection microwave or your conventional oven and your microwave as a team.)

2 cups saskatoons	1 tablespoon lemon juice
1 cup water	1 tablespoon butter or
1 cup sugar	margarine
2 tablespoons cornstarch	Pastry dough for 9-inch
dissolved in 2	two-crust pie (see page
tablespoons water	189)

1. Combine saskatoons and water in a 2-quart microwave-safe bowl. Cover loosely with plastic wrap. Microwave for 3 to 4 minutes at HIGH (100%) or until boiling.
2. Blend in sugar and dissolved cornstarch; cover again. Microwave for 2 to 3 minutes at high (100%) or until boiling and thickened, stirring twice. Stir in lemon juice.

3. Pour filling into one pastry-lined glass microwave-safe and oven-safe pie plate; dot with butter. Roll out remaining dough for top crust and drape it over the pie. Crimp edges and cut several vents in the top.

4. Preheat oven to 400°F.

   For convection microwave: Low-Mix Bake at 400°F. on a raised rack for 35 minutes or until crust is browned (or use Code #2 or Combination #2 for 35 minutes).

   For microwave and a regular oven: Microwave for 9 to 10 minutes at HIGH (100%). Transfer to your regular oven (preheated) and bake for 10 to 15 minutes or until crust is browned. Shield crimped edge with foil during oven baking if it starts to overcook. Let stand on counter until cool.

Yield: 1 9-inch pie.

———————— · ❄ · ————————

Variation: For Raisin Pie: Substitute raisins for saskatoons. Proceed as directed.

Variation: For Blueberry (double crust) Pie: Substitute 4 cups cleaned blueberries for the 2 cups saskatoons and 3 tablespoons flour for the 2 tablespoons cornstarch. Omit water and steps #1 and #2. Combine blueberries with sugar, flour, and lemon juice to make the filling. Proceed as directed in steps #3, #4, and #5.

CHOCOLATE AND STRAWBERRIES TRUFFLE PIE

—————— • • • • • ——————

TIPS
....

I love to serve this pie for dessert at dinner parties. My guests seem to love it, too!

To make this pie even easier, use a store-bought vanilla crust.

·················· FILLING ··················

2 tablespoons butter or margarine

⅔ cup semisweet chocolate chips

8-ounce package cream cheese

3 tablespoons orange-flavored liqueur or orange juice

½ cup powdered sugar

9-inch vanilla wafer or baked pastry crust (see pages 187, 189)

3 cups whole strawberries, washed and stems removed (1½ pounds)

·················· GLAZE ··················

⅓ cup red currant jelly

·················· GARNISH ··················

1 cup (2 ounces) whipped topping plus extra berries

1. **Filling:** Microwave butter, chocolate chips, and cream cheese in a 2-quart microwave-safe bowl for 2 to 3 minutes at MEDIUM HIGH (70%). Stir until smooth and melted. Blend in orange liqueur and powdered sugar; mix well.
2. Pour into prepared crust. Cool slightly.
3. Gently press strawberries into chocolate filling.
4. **Glaze:** Microwave jelly in a custard cup for 60 to 90 seconds at HIGH (100%), or until melted. Brush berries with jelly glaze. Refrigerate at least 2 hours before serving (or freeze 1 hour). Serve each slice garnished with

whipped topping and a strawberry (or chocolate-tipped strawberry; see page 100), if desired.

Yield: 1 9-inch pie.

———————— · ❄ · ————————

Variation: Individual Truffle Cups: Omit crust. Place 2 paper baking cups in each of 8 cups of a muffin pan or in 8 custard cups. Place a vanilla (cookie) wafer in each cup. Distribute cooked filling among cups. Press 1 strawberry in each cup. Glaze. Chill.

TIPS
....

For Quick Strawberry Mellow Pie: Substitute 2 cups sliced fresh strawberries for the red raspberries.

QUICK RED RASPBERRY MELLOW PIE

———————— · · · · · · ————————

5 cups miniature marshmallows (or 55 large)
½ cup milk
2 cups (8 ounces) whipped topping

2 cups fresh red raspberries
9-inch graham cracker crust (see page 187)

1. Combine marshmallows and milk in a 2-quart microwave- and freezer-safe bowl. Microwave for 2½ to 3 minutes at HIGH (100%). Stir until mixture is smooth.
2. Place in freezer for 15 to 20 minutes until slightly thickened.
3. Fold in whipped topping and berries. Spoon into crust. Refrigerate at least 2 hours or overnight. Serve garnished with additional whipped topping, if desired.

Yield: 1 9-inch pie.

———————— · ❄ · ————————

....

Common sense is the knack of seeing things as they are and doing things as they ought to be done.

RHUBARB CREAM PIE

. . . . .

3 cups fresh diced rhubarb
1 cup boiling water
2 medium eggs, separated
1¼ cups sugar, divided
Dash of salt
2 tablespoons cornstarch
¼ teaspoon cinnamon

¼ teaspoon nutmeg
1 teaspoon vanilla
⅓ cup half-and-half
1 baked pie crust (baked
  in a glass or microwave-
  safe pie plate)

1. Cover rhubarb with boiling water. Let stand 10 minutes,
   then drain. Set aside.
2. Beat egg whites until stiff, adding ¼ cup of the sugar.
   Set aside. Combine egg yolks, salt, cornstarch, spices, vanilla, and half-and-half in a large bowl and beat well. Stir
   in rhubarb. Fold in egg whites. Pour into the pie crust.
3. Microwave for 30 to 35 minutes at MEDIUM (50%).
   Cool to set before serving.

Yield: 1 9-inch pie.

. ❄ .

AMERICAN KEY LIME PIE

. . . . .

1 envelope unflavored
  gelatin
⅓ cup water
4 large egg yolks, beaten
½ cup lime juice
⅔ cup sugar
Dash of salt
1 teaspoon grated lime
  peel (zest only)
¼ teaspoon green food
  coloring (optional)

1⅔ cups (4 ounces)
  whipped topping or 2
  cups whipped cream
9-inch graham cracker or
  pretzel pie crust (see
  page 187)
Additional whipped
  topping and grated lime
  peel or pistachio nuts to
  garnish (optional)

TIPS
. . . .

To keep the filling from
leaking through a
baked pie crust: After
baking or microwaving
crust, brush crust with
one lightly beaten egg
yolk to seal prick holes.
Microwave for 30 to
40 seconds to set.

Grate lime zest as you
would lemon zest. See
(Lemon Bars Deluxe)
tip on page 39.

1. Mix gelatin and water; set aside. Beat yolks, lime juice, sugar, and salt in a 2-quart microwave-safe bowl until foamy. Beat in gelatin and water. Microwave for 2 to 3 minutes at HIGH (100%), until boiling, stirring once. Stir in grated lime peel and food coloring, if desired.
2. Chill, stirring occasionally, until mixture mounds slightly and resembles the consistency of mayonnaise. Fold in whipped topping. Pile into prepared pie crust. Chill until firm. Serve garnished with additional whipped topping and grated lime peel or pistachio nuts.

Yield: 1 9-inch pie.

———————— · ❄ · ————————

Variation: Orange Citrus Pie: Use a baked pastry crust. Substitute ½ cup orange juice and ⅓ cup lemon juice for the lime juice and water. Substitute ½ teaspoon orange peel and ½ teaspoon lemon peel for the lime peel. Garnish with additional whipped topping and thin orange slices, cut in fourths.

OPEN BLUEBERRY PIE
———————— · · · · · ————————

The fresh berry taste is fabulous!

4–5 cups fresh or frozen blueberries	1 baked pie shell or vanilla wafer crust (see page 187)
1 cup sugar	1 cup (2 ounces) whipped topping to garnish (optional)
½ cup water	
3 tablespoons cornstarch	
1 tablespoon butter	

1. Mash ½ cup of blueberries in a 2-quart microwave-safe bowl. Add sugar and ¼ cup water to the mashed berries. Microwave for 2 to 3 minutes at HIGH (100%), until boiling.

TIPS
·······

I used to live in northern Minnesota where the blueberries were plentiful. My friends and I would often go blueberry picking in the woods. Open Blueberry Pie was our favorite treat to make with these hand-picked delicacies.

When blueberries aren't as plentiful, try substituting strawberries or red raspberries. They will also make a delicious, fresh-tasting pie.

2. In a separate dish, combine cornstarch and ¼ cup water. Add to boiling mixture. Microwave for 1 to 2 minutes at HIGH (100%), until thick. Add butter; stir until melted. Cool and/or refrigerate.

3. Before serving, fold in the remaining blueberries and pile into the baked or prepared pie crust. Serve garnished with whipped topping.

Yield: 1 9-inch pie.

———————— · ❄ · ————————

FRESH PEACH PIE

An easy, fresh-tasting pie for a warm summer day!

5–6 cups sliced, peeled fresh peaches (about 6 peaches)
¾ cup sugar
¾ cup water
3 tablespoons orange juice concentrate
¼ cup cornstarch

9-inch baked pie shell, or graham cracker, or vanilla wafer crust (see pages 188–189, 187)
1 cup (2 ounces) whipped topping plus peach slices to garnish (optional)

1. Mash 1 cup of peaches in a 2-quart microwave-safe bowl. Refrigerate remainder.

2. Stir in sugar, water, orange juice concentrate, and cornstarch until well blended. Microwave for 5 to 6 minutes at HIGH (100%), until thickened, stirring once. Cool. Fold in remaining peaches.

3. Pour into the prepared crust. Refrigerate 1½ to 2 hours until set. Serve each slice topped with a dollop of whipped topping and a peach slice, if desired.

Yield: 1 9-inch pie.

———————— · ❄ · ————————

The world is full of willing people—some willing to work and others willing to let them.

TIPS
....

For a Peaches and Cream Pie: Make the white layer of the Independence Day Pie on page 179. Pour it into the pie crust and top with the fresh Peach Pie filling as directed here.

GRAHAM CRACKER CRUST
(WITH VARIATIONS)

——————— · · · · · ———————

1½ cups crushed graham crackers (or variations, see below)

¼ cup sugar
1 stick (1 cup) butter or margarine, softened

1. Microwave butter for 20 to 30 seconds at HIGH (100%) to soften. Mix all ingredients together.
2. Press into a 9- or 10-inch microwave-safe pie plate. Microwave for 1 to 1½ minutes at MEDIUM HIGH (70%).

Yield: 1 9- or 10-inch pie crust.

——————— · ❄ · ———————

.... VARIATIONS ....

Chocolate Cookie Crust: Substitute 1½ cups crushed whole Oreo cookies or chocolate wafers for graham crackers. Refrigerate instead of microwaving in step #2.

Vanilla Wafer Crust: Substitute 1½ cups crushed vanilla wafers or gingersnaps for graham crackers.

Pretzel Crust: Substitute 1¼ cups coarsely crushed pretzels for graham crackers.

Corn Flake or Cereal Crust: Substitute 1¼ cups corn flake crumbs or crisp rice cereal for graham crackers.

TOASTED COCONUT AND
TOASTED COCONUT CRUST

——————— · · · · · ———————

1¼ cups flaked coconut
½ stick (¼ cup) butter or margarine

¼ cup sugar

Anytime you use a recipe that calls for toasted coconut, simply follow step #1 of this recipe.

1. **To toast coconut:** Microwave flaked coconut in a thin layer on a paper plate or pie plate for 4 to 5 minutes at MEDIUM HIGH (70%), or until coconut starts to turn light brown, stirring every minute until toasted. (It will continue to brown for 1 minute after microwaving.) Set aside.
2. Microwave butter for 10 to 15 seconds at HIGH (100%). Stir in sugar and toasted coconut.
3. Press into a 9-inch microwave pie plate. Microwave for 1 minute at MEDIUM HIGH (70%) to set.

Yield: 1 9-inch pie crust.

———————— · ❊ · ————————

BEST BAKED PIE CRUST

————— · · · · · —————

Use your conventional oven for this one!

1½ cups flour
1 tablespoon powdered
  sugar (optional)
½ teaspoon salt
½ cup plus 2 tablespoons
  butter-flavored solid
  shortening

2 tablespoons cold water
1½ teaspoons white
  vinegar
1 small egg

1. Preheat conventional oven to 400°F. Using a food processor or pastry blender and bowl, blend flour, sugar (optional), salt, and shortening until mixture is very crumbly.
2. Mix cold water, vinegar, and egg in a small bowl. Add to crumbly mixture; mix until dough forms a ball using a food processor or fork. Cover with plastic wrap and freeze 5 to 10 minutes.
3. Roll out pie crust between two pieces of waxed paper to fill a 9- or 10-inch glass microwave-safe and oven-safe pie

TIPS

This is my all-time favorite never-fail pie crust recipe. It's made in the conventional oven instead of the microwave oven. Use this recipe whenever a baked pie crust is required.

If you have the time use your conventional oven to make this baked pie crust as the flavor and crispness of this crust cannot be duplicated in a microwave oven.

If you don't have the time to use your conventional oven, see page 189 for microwave pie crusts.

plate. Flute edges and prick bottom and sides to prevent bubbling when baking.

4. Bake at 400°F. for 15 to 18 minutes or until lightly browned.

Yield: 1 baked 9- or 10-inch pie crust.*

———————— · ❄ · ————————

Variation: For Unbaked Pie Shell: Proceed as directed through step #3. Omit step #4.

Variation: For Pastry Dough for 9-inch or 10-inch **Double Crust Pie (unbaked):** Double the ingredients. Proceed as directed through step #3.

EASY MICROWAVE-BAKED PIE CRUSTS

———————— · · · · · ————————

·················· **BASIC PIE CRUST** ··················

2 cups flour	¾ cup solid shortening
1 teaspoon salt	6 tablespoons iced water or tea

·················· **FRENCH PASTRY** ··················

2 cups flour	1 stick (½ cup) butter or margarine
1 teaspoon sugar	1 small egg, beaten (2 tablespoons) mixed with 4 tablespoons iced water or tea
1 teaspoon salt	
¼ cup solid shortening	

1. **Basic and French:** Blend flour, (plus sugar), salt, and shortening (plus butter) together in a bowl until mixture

··
*For two crusts, double the ingredients and proceed as directed.

is very crumbly. Use a food processor or pastry blender.
2. Mix iced water (and egg); add to crumbly mixture. Mix until dough forms a ball.
3. Divide in half and refrigerate at least 15 minutes.
4. Roll out pie crust to fit a 9-inch microwave-safe pie plate. Flute edges and prick bottom and sides to prevent bubbling when cooking. Place on an inverted saucer in the microwave oven.
5. Microwave for 6 to 8 minutes at MEDIUM HIGH (70%),* or just until brown spots appear, rotating plate and reshaping fluted edges every two minutes.

Yield: 2 baked 9-inch pie crusts.

———————— · ❄ · ————————

For a pretty and shiny crust and/or to seal prick holes in a crust to be filled with a custard-type filling: Brush crust with 1 beaten egg or egg yolk the last 30 to 40 seconds of microwaving time.

F R O Z E N   P I E   C R U S T

——————— · · · · · ———————

Purchased from frozen-food section of any grocery store.

1 deep dish frozen pie crust

1. Spray a glass or microwave-safe pie plate with vegetable shortening.
2. Remove frozen crust from foil pie plate and place in microwave-safe pie plate. Let stand at room temperature for 10 to 20 minutes to defrost. Shape crust to fit pie plate. Prick sides and bottom. Place on an inverted saucer in the microwave oven.
3. Microwave for 4 to 5 minutes at HIGH (100%), rotating plate and reshaping edges every two minutes.

Yield: 1 baked 9-inch pie crust.

——————— · ❄ · ———————

*Compacts: Microwave for 5 to 7 minutes at HIGH (100%).

HOLIDAY PICKLES, PRESERVES, AND GIFT IDEAS

· ❄ ·

TIPS

You can substitute 2 cups of cranberry juice and 1½ cups of apple juice for the cranapple juice.

Add 1 or 2 drops of food coloring to step #2 to enhance the red coloring of the jelly, if desired.

Microwaved jellies made with sugar will keep up to four months in the refrigerator.

CRANAPPLE JELLY

· · · · ·

Makes a "sweet" Christmas gift!

3½ cups cranapple juice beverage
1¾-ounce package powdered pectin

3 cups sugar
Red food coloring (optional)

1. Combine juice and pectin in a 2-quart microwave-safe bowl, stirring until pectin is dissolved. Microwave for 10

to 12 minutes, uncovered, at HIGH (100%), until mixture boils, stirring every 3 minutes.

2. Stir in sugar. Microwave for 6 to 7 minutes at HIGH (100%), until mixture starts to boil again. Microwave for 1 minute longer while mixture is boiling.
3. Skim off foam. Pour into hot sterilized jars or mugs, cover, cool, and refrigerate or freeze or seal with Frothy Paraffin, if desired (see page 193) or in the usual boiling water bath manner.

Yield: 5 cups.

———————— · ❄ · ————————

Variation: Christmas party favors or gifts: Cool jelly slightly; pour into inexpensive goblets or plastic champagne glasses. Cover with plastic wrap and secure with a piece of yarn or a ribbon and a bow. Store in the refrigerator.

GRAPE JELLY
(OR APPLE, PEAR, OR PINEAPPLE)

———————— · · · · · ————————

Pour into a mug or decorative jar for a nice gift.

6-ounce can frozen grape juice concentrate (or apple, pineapple, etc.), thawed

2 cups water
1¾ ounce package powdered pectin
3⅔ cups sugar

1. Combine juice and water in a 2-quart microwave-safe bowl. Stir in pectin until dissolved.
2. Microwave for 10 to 12 minutes at HIGH (100%), until boiling. Stir every 3 minutes during cooking.
3. Stir in sugar.
4. Microwave for 6 to 7 minutes at HIGH (100%), until mixture starts to boil again, stirring twice to prevent boilovers. Microwave for 1 minute longer at HIGH (100%) while mixture is boiling.

TIPS
········

An extra 6-ounce can of frozen juice you have on hand, some powdered pectin, and sugar make seven to eight small jars of delicious jam.

Use Sure-Jell brand, if possible, for the powdered pectin.

5. Skim off foam. Pour into hot sterilized jars or mugs. Cover and let stand at room temperature to cool. Refrigerate or freeze.

Yield:. 4 cups or 7 to 8 small jars.

———————— · ❄ · ————————

TIPS
....

Frothy Paraffin Snow will top and decorate mugs of jelly so they resemble frothy drinks.

DO NOT microwave paraffin. Paraffin is impervious to microwaves and will not melt in the microwave oven. Use the stovetop and a double boiler to melt paraffin.

FROTHY PARAFFIN SNOW TO DECORATE AND TOP JAMS AND JELLIES

——————— · · · · · ———————

2 bars paraffin

1. Pour jelly into a decorative mug or glass.
2. Melt paraffin in a double boiler or in a jar immersed in a pan of 2 inches of boiling water. Cover mugs with a thin layer of melted paraffin to seal jelly or jam.
3. Cool paraffin slightly until cloudy.
4. With an electric mixer, beat paraffin until foamy; spoon over mugs. Work quickly so mixture doesn't harden. Refrigerate jelly.

Yield: Frothy paraffin for 6 mugs or glasses.

———————— · ❄ · ————————

. . . .
Those who wish to sing always find a song.

F R E S H   P E A R   J A M

———————— · · · · · ————————

You can substitute any fresh fruit.

2 cups fresh, peeled,
  cored, and finely
  chopped pears

3 tablespoons powdered
  pectin
2 cups sugar
2 teaspoons lemon juice

1. With a fork, crush fruit in a 2-quart microwave-safe bowl. Microwave for 3 minutes at HIGH (100%).
2. Stir in pectin. Microwave for 2 minutes at HIGH (100%), or until bubbly.
3. Stir in sugar and lemon juice.
4. Microwave for 6 to 7 minutes at HIGH (100%).*
5. Pour into sterilized jars. Cover and let stand at room temperature to cool. Refrigerate or freeze.

Yield: 2½ cups or 3 to 4 small jars.

———————— · ❄ · ————————

B I L L I E ' S   F A V O R I T E
S T R A W B E R R Y - R H U B A R B   A N D
P I N E A P P L E   J A M

———————— · · · · · ————————

5 cups thinly sliced fresh
  rhubarb
4 cups sugar
8½-ounce can crushed
  pineapple, undrained

3-ounce package
  strawberry or raspberry
  gelatin, dry

You can substitute any fruit for the pears. Start with approximately 1 pound of fresh fruit before preparation.

Microwaved jams will keep up to two months in the refrigerator.

This jam recipe is one I adapted from a recipe Billie Oakley shared on her radio show. (Billie is a friend of mine who hosted a daily talk show from Shenandoah, Iowa. Her radio show is aired throughout the Midwest.)

···
*Compacts: Microwave at HIGH (100%) for 8 minutes.

Heat this jam for 20 to 30 seconds at HIGH (100%), and serve it as a topping on ice cream, cheese cake, pancakes, or angel food cake. On ice cream and with a few banana slices, the flavor resembles a banana split.

TIPS
....

For Orange-Zucchini Marmalade: Substitute 2½ cups peeled and grated zucchini for the pears. Proceed as directed.

1. Combine rhubarb and sugar in a 2-quart or larger bowl. Let stand at least 2 hours (overnight is best) so that the rhubarb makes its own juice.
2. Microwave rhubarb-sugar mixture for 25 minutes at HIGH (100%), stirring three times while cooking. Add pineapple. Microwave 4 to 5 minutes longer at HIGH (100%).
3. Stir in gelatin. Mix well.
4. Pour into sterilized jars. Cover and let stand at room temperature to cool. Store in the refrigerator or freezer.

Yield: 3 cups or 3 to 4 small jars.

———————— · ❄ · ————————

ORANGE-PEAR MARMALADE
(WITH ZUCCHINI MARMALADE VARIATION)

———————— · · · · · ————————

3 cups peeled, chopped pears (4–5)

1 orange, unpeeled, and grated or ground in a food processor or grinder

2¼ cups sugar

¼ cup frozen orange juice concentrate (almost ½ of 6-ounce can), thawed

2 teaspoons lemon juice

3-ounce package orange gelatin, dry

1. Combine chopped pears, grated orange, sugar, orange juice concentrate, and lemon juice in a 2-quart microwave-safe bowl. Microwave, uncovered, for 20 to 22 minutes at HIGH (100%), or until orange peel is translucent and mixture boils well, stirring twice.
2. Stir in gelatin. Microwave for 1 to 2 minutes until mixture boils again. Pour into sterilized jars. Seal and let stand at room temperature to cool. Store in the refrigerator or freezer. Jam thickens when cooled.

Yield: 3 cups or 3 to 4 small jars.

———————— · ❄ · ————————

PICKLES

REFRIGERATOR PICKLES
———— · · · * · · ————

7 cups thinly sliced
   cucumbers (unpeeled)
1 cup sliced onions
1 cup sliced green pepper
   (optional)
1 tablespoon pickling salt

2 cups sugar
1 cup white or cider
   vinegar
1 tablespoon celery seed
1 teaspoon mustard seed
   (optional)

1. Combine cucumbers, onion, green pepper (optional), and pickling salt. Cover and let stand 1 hour.
2. Combine sugar, vinegar, and seeds in a 1-quart microwave-safe bowl. Microwave for 8 to 10 minutes at HIGH (100%), or until boiling.
3. Drain cucumbers well. Pour slightly cooled vinegar syrup over cucumbers. Refrigerate in a covered container for at least three days.

Yield: 2 quarts.

———— · ❄ · ————

BREAD AND BUTTER PICKLES
———— · · · · · ————

2 quarts (8 cups) thinly
   sliced cucumbers
3 medium white onions,
   thinly sliced
1 clove garlic
1 red or green pepper,
   seeded and cut into
   narrow strips
¼ cup canning salt

4 cups water and cracked
   ice (mixed)
1½ cups sugar
1½ cups cider or white
   vinegar
2 teaspoons mustard seed
½ teaspoon celery seed
½ teaspoon turmeric
   powder
Dash of ground cloves

Pickles will be ready to eat in three days. They can be kept in the refrigerator for up to four months.

The microwave oven is especially handy when it comes to preserving small amounts of food from backyard gardens or end-of-summer produce.

For larger quantities, however, conventional cooking methods still work the best.

Do NOT try to can in your microwave unless you use a special microwave canner (purchased in a microwave accessory store).

1. Combine cucumbers, onions, garlic, pepper, salt, and iced water. Let stand 3 hours. Drain thoroughly.
2. Combine remaining ingredients and drained vegetables in a 3-quart microwave-safe bowl. Microwave for 22 to 28 minutes at HIGH (100%), until onions are almost translucent, stirring twice. Spoon into sterilized pint jars, filling liquid to ½ inch from top of jar. Seal and process in boiling water bath for 10 minutes. Cool and store.

Yield: 4 pints.

— · ❄ · —

DILL PICKLES

· · · · ·

······················ PICKLES ·······················

3–6 cloves garlic (½–1 per jar)
6 sprigs of fresh dill

3 teaspoons pickling spice (½ teaspoon per jar)
40 (3-inch) cucumbers for pickling, washed and prepared

······················ BRINE ·······················

¼ teaspoon alum
3 cups water

1½ cups vinegar
⅓ cup pickling salt

1. **Pickles:** Fill sterilized jars with garlic, dill, pickling spice, and cucumbers, divided evenly among the jars. Set aside.
2. **Brine:** Combine brine ingredients in a 2-quart microwave-safe bowl. Microwave for 11 to 12 minutes at HIGH (100%), or until boiling.
3. Pour brine over cucumbers. Seal using the conventional boiling water bath for 10 minutes or refrigerate. If refrigerated, pickles are ready in one week and can be kept for three months.

Yield: 6 pints.

— · ❄ · —

DISPENSER LIQUID SOAP

————— · · · · · —————

4½–5 ounces grated   3½ cups water
  moisturizing soap

1. Microwave moisturizing soap and water for 6 to 7 minutes at HIGH (100%), stirring two to three times.
2. Cool to thicken. Pour into dispensers.

Yield: Approximately 4 cups.

————— · ❄ · —————

You can use up to 3 ounces of your leftover soap bits and pieces for part of the moisturizing soap. Be sure to weigh the soap on a small kitchen scale.

DRIED ORANGE, LEMON, TANGERINE, OR LIME PEEL

————— · · · · · —————

Great to have on hand for garnishing and flavoring.

2 large citrus fruits
  (oranges, lemons,
  tangerines, or limes),
  washed and patted dry

1. Finely grate the zest from the citrus fruits. Spread on two layers of paper toweling. Microwave for 1 to 1½ minutes at HIGH (100%).
2. Stir and rearrange. Microwave again for 1 to 2 minutes at HIGH (100%), or until slightly dried. Let stand and cool until dry, about 2 hours. Store in an airtight container.

Yield: ½ cup dried peel.

————— · ❄ · —————

See tip for grating the zest of citrus fruit on page 39.

Substitute 1 teaspoon dried peel for 1 tablespoon fresh peel in any recipe.

A good laugh is sunshine in a house.

TIPS
········

Although a food de-hydrator works best for drying large quantities of fruit, you can use your microwave oven to dry some fruits quickly. Since only some of the moisture evaporates during the microwaving time, be sure to allow the fruit to continue to dry out on the wire rack over-night.

When drying fruits or herbs, do only ten batches or fewer at a time. (This will prevent the magnetron tube in your microwave oven from overheating.)

DRIED BANANAS, APPLES, PINEAPPLE, OR APRICOTS

——————— · · · · · ———————

2 ripe bananas, or 2
  Delicious apples, or 1
  whole pineapple; or 16-
  ounce can apricot
  halves; or 20-ounce can
  pineapple rings

1. Prepare fruit: Peel and slice bananas ¼ inch thick; or peel, core, and slice apples ¼ inch thick; or quarter, cut out core, and remove fruit from the fresh pineapple, then slice ¼ inch thick; or drain canned apricots or pineapple rings and blot dry with paper toweling.
2. Arrange slices of prepared fruit on a microwave roasting rack. Do not overlap pieces. Microwave 1 roasting rack of fruit for 15 to 20 minutes at MEDIUM (50%).* (Bananas will be slightly sticky to the touch; apples, pineapple slices, and apricots will look very limp and slightly moist.) Remove to wire rack and let stand overnight. Store in an airtight container.

Yield: 1 cup dried fruit.

——————— · ❄ · ———————

···
*Note: Apricots may take up to 25 to 30 minutes at MEDIUM (50%).

DRIED HERBS FROM THE MICROWAVE OVEN

————————— • • • • • —————————

1 cup (not packed) or
  about 6 sprigs of
  parsley, sage, dill,
  rosemary, etc.

1. Rinse and thoroughly dry herbs.
2. Place herbs on a microwave-safe rack or plate that has
   been lined with two layers of paper towels.
   Arrange in a ring or circle and cover with a paper towel.
3. Microwave for 2½ to 3½ minutes at HIGH (100%). Cool
   completely. Store in an airtight container.

Yield: ⅓ to ½ cup dried herbs.

————————— • ❋ • —————————

TIPS
....

The quickest and easi-
est way to dry your
windowsill or backyard
produce is to use your
microwave.

One teaspoon dried
herbs can be sub-
stituted for 1 table-
spoon fresh herbs in
most recipes.

HOLIDAY EGGS AND BRUNCH

· ❄ ·

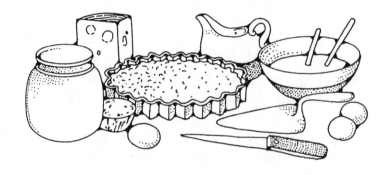

SAUSAGE AND SPINACH FRITTATA

· · · · ·

TIPS

For tips on making your own dry bread crumbs, see page 56.

You can omit the chopped celery, if desired.

10-ounce box frozen, chopped spinach
1 pound bulk pork sausage, crumbled
½ cup chopped onion
½ cup chopped celery
¾ cup dry bread crumbs

½ cup (two ounces) shredded Cheddar, Swiss, or Monterey Jack cheese
½ teaspoon ground sage
2 medium eggs, well beaten
1 cup (4 ounces) shredded Cheddar cheese
Parsley sprigs or chopped pimiento to garnish (optional)

1. Microwave spinach in box for 5 minutes at HIGH (100%). Drain and set aside.

2. Crumble sausage in a 9- or 10-inch microwave-safe or glass pie plate. Add onion and celery and cover with a paper towel. Microwave for 4 to 5 minutes at HIGH (100%), until no longer pink. Drain off fat.

3. Stir in bread crumbs, ½ cup cheese, sage, and eggs. Stir in spinach. Mix well.

4. Microwave for 11 to 12 minutes at MEDIUM (50%), until set. Sprinkle with Cheddar cheese. Let stand 5 minutes. Serve in wedges garnished with parsley and chopped pimiento.

Yield: 4 to 5 servings.

———————— · ❈ · ————————

EASY CHEESY HAM AND EGG MUFFIN BREAKFAST

················· SAUCE ·················

3 tablespoons milk
1½ cups (6 ounces) processed cheese spread, grated or cubed

2½-ounce jar chopped mushrooms, drained (optional)
1 tablespoon chopped pimiento (optional)

················· HAM AND EGG MIXTURE ·················

3 large eggs, beaten
3 tablespoons milk (or water)
6 slices cooked ham (1 ounce each)

3 English muffins, split, toasted, and buttered (use raisin, wheat, or white)
1 tablespoon chopped parsley or chives

1. Sauce: Microwave milk and cheese in a 1-quart microwave-safe bowl for 2 to 3 minutes at MEDIUM HIGH

TIPS
········

For a terrific brunch idea, try an Egg Muffin with Broccoli or Asparagus: Microwave a 10-ounce box of frozen broccoli or asparagus for 5½ to 6 minutes at HIGH (100%). Drain. When assembling breakfast in step #4, top each ham slice with one or two spears of broccoli or asparagus. Add eggs and sauce and proceed as directed.

(70%). Stir until smooth. Stir in mushrooms and/or pimiento, if desired. Set aside.

2. **Ham and Egg Mixture:** Combine eggs and milk in a 1-
quart microwave-safe casserole. Microwave for 2½ to 3½
minutes at MEDIUM HIGH (70%), or until eggs are not
quite set (still moist on top), stirring twice.

3. Microwave ham slices on a paper plate and wrapped in a
paper towel or waxed paper, for 1 to 2 minutes at HIGH
(100%), until very hot.

4. Assemble breakfast: Top each buttered muffin half with a
ham slice (fold in half if too large); spoon eggs over ham;
top with sauce. Garnish with chopped parsley. Microwave
1 to 2 minutes at HIGH (100%) on a microwave-safe
serving plate, until hot. Serve immediately.

Yield: 4 to 6 servings.

———————— · ❄ · ————————

SAUSAGE BREAKFAST WEDGES

————————— · · · · · —————————

½-pound bulk pork
  sausage
Browning powder for
  meat (optional), onion
  and garlic flavored
1 cup (4 ounces) shredded
  Cheddar or American
  cheese
2 tablespoons diced onion

¾ cup milk
4 large eggs, beaten
1 teaspoon dried parsley,
  or 2 tablespoons
  chopped fresh parsley
2 tablespoons butter,
  sliced

1. Crumble sausage in a 9-inch microwave-safe pie plate.
Sprinkle with browning powder, if desired. Cover with a
paper towel. Microwave for 3 to 4 minutes at HIGH
(100%), until no longer pink. Drain off fat.

· ·

Stumbling blocks make good stepping-stones.

2. Sprinkle cheese over sausage. Stir in onion.
3. In a medium-size bowl, combine milk and eggs. Add parsley and butter. Pour over sausage. Cover with plastic wrap. Microwave for 4 minutes at HIGH (100%). Stir. Cover again. Microwave for 6 to 8 minutes at MEDIUM (50%), until center is almost set. Let stand covered for 5 minutes. Serve in wedges garnished with parsley.

Yield: 4 servings.

———— · ❈ · ————

BLENDER EASY EGG OMELET

12 large eggs
1 teaspoon seasoned salt
1 cup milk
8-ounce package cream
    cheese or Neufchatel
    cheese, cut into ¼-inch
    slices

Chopped parsley or grated
    Cheddar cheese to
    garnish, optional

T I P S
....

For a special holiday breakfast or brunch omelet, add 1 cup diced cooked ham to the egg mixture before adding the cheese in step #2.

1. Using a blender, blend eggs, seasoned salt, and milk for 30 seconds, until light and foamy. Pour into a greased 9- or 10-inch microwave-safe casserole.
2. Slide cream cheese slices into egg mixture. Cover with lid or plastic wrap (vent one edge). Microwave for 2 minutes at MEDIUM HIGH (70%); gently stir. Cover again. Microwave for 6 to 8 minutes at MEDIUM HIGH (70%), or until almost set (lift slightly twice during microwaving to let uncooked part run to sides).
3. Sprinkle with parsley or Cheddar cheese to garnish, if desired. Let stand covered for 3 minutes. Cut in wedges or squares and serve immediately.

Yield: 6 to 8 servings.

———— · ❈ · ————

The priceless ingredient of any recipe is a good cook.

One 4-ounce can sliced mushrooms, drained well, can be added with the cheese in step #1, if desired.

One 4-ounce can sliced mushrooms, drained well, can be added with the cheese in step #1, if desired.

QUICHE LORRAINE

(WITH SALMON QUICHE VARIATION)

—————— · · · · · ——————

8–10 slices bacon
1½ cups (6 ounces) Swiss
  or Cheddar cheese,
  shredded
¼ cup onion, diced
9-inch baked pastry crust
  (see pages 188–189)

1¼ cups evaporated milk
  or half-and-half
4 medium eggs, beaten
Dash of salt and pepper

1. Microwave bacon between two double layers of paper towels on a microwave-safe dish or paper plate for 1 minute per slice at HIGH (100%). Cool slightly; crumble. Sprinkle bacon, cheese, and onion into the cooled pie crust.
2. In a microwave-safe bowl, beat milk, eggs, and seasonings until well blended. Microwave for 4 to 5 minutes at HIGH (100%), until slightly thickened, stirring twice. Pour over bacon-cheese mixture. Place on inverted saucer in oven.
3. Microwave for 18 to 20 minutes at MEDIUM (50%),* until center is almost set, rotating dish twice if necessary for even cooking. Let stand 5 minutes.

Yield: 5 to 6 servings.

—————— · ❋ · ——————

Variation: Salmon Quiche: Substitute 7¾-ounce can salmon for the crumbled bacon. Add a dash of dry mustard, if desired.

....

*Compacts: Microwave quiche for 15 to 16 minutes at HIGH (100%) in step #3.

....

When you know all the answers, you haven't asked all the questions.

CHEDDAR STRATA

. . . . .

Make it the night before!

1 tablespoon butter or
  margarine, divided
⅓ cup chopped onion
¼ teaspoon marjoram
4-ounce can sliced
  mushrooms, drained
5 slices buttered bread,
  crusts removed

1 cup (4 ounces) shredded
  Cheddar cheese
2 tablespoons Parmesan
  cheese
4 large eggs, beaten
1 cup milk
Dash of salt and pepper

1. Mix butter and onion in a large custard cup. Cover with plastic wrap. Microwave for 2½ to 3 minutes at HIGH (100%), until onions are tender. Stir in marjoram and mushrooms. Set aside.

2. Cut bread into ½-inch cubes. Arrange half the cubes in bottom of 4 custard cups or individual casserole dishes (10 ounces each). Top each with mushroom-onion mixture. Top with Cheddar cheese and sprinkle with Parmesan. Top with remaining bread cubes.

3. Combine eggs, milk, salt, and pepper. Pour over bread cubes in each custard cup. Refrigerate overnight, covered.

4. The next day, microwave each dish, covered with waxed paper, for 2 to 2½ minutes at MEDIUM HIGH (70%).

For 4 dishes: Arrange in a circle. Microwave for 4 minutes at MEDIUM HIGH (70%). (Rotate dishes and move each to a different spot.) Microwave again for 5 to 6 minutes at MEDIUM HIGH (70%). Let stand 3 minutes.

Yield: 4 servings.

❄

The glory of every morning is that it offers us a chance to begin again.

You can substitute brown sugar for the white sugar in the apple layer. Sometimes I like to use ¼ cup white sugar and ¼ cup brown sugar in place of the ½ cup sugar.

You can substitute 1 cup of any pancake batter for the batter in step #2.

DELICIOUS APPLE PANCAKE

──────── • • • • ────────

Serve as a delightful breakfast treat or top with ice cream for a fun dessert!

.... APPLE LAYER ....

3 tablespoons butter or margarine
½ cup sugar

1 medium apple, peeled and thinly sliced
½ teaspoon cinnamon

.... BATTER ....

1 cup buttermilk baking mix

1 medium egg
½ cup milk

.... TOPPING ....

2 teaspoons sugar

¼ teaspoon cinnamon

1. **Apple Layer:** Microwave butter in a 9-inch microwave-safe baking dish for 30 seconds at HIGH (100%). Stir in sugar, apple, and cinnamon. Cover with plastic wrap and microwave for 3½ to 5 minutes at HIGH (100%), until apples are tender. Set aside.
2. **Batter:** Combine all the batter ingredients with an electric mixer until smooth; pour over the cooked apple slices.
3. **Topping:** Combine topping ingredients and sprinkle over batter. Microwave for 4 to 5 minutes at HIGH (100%). Let stand 5 minutes. Serve topped with a pat of butter or lightly drizzled with pancake syrup, if desired.

Yield: 4 servings.

──────── • ❄ • ────────

EASY SAUSAGE BRUNCH

10-ounce package frozen
  hash browns
12 ounces bulk sausage,
  crumbled
1 medium onion, chopped
½ cup dry bread crumbs

1½ cups (6 ounces)
  shredded Cheddar
  cheese, divided
Dash of salt and pepper
2 eggs, beaten
1 tomato or parsley sprigs
  to garnish, optional

1. Microwave frozen hash browns in the package on a paper towel for 3 to 4 minutes at HIGH (100%). Set aside.
2. Microwave sausage and onion in a 9-inch microwave-safe pie plate, covered with a paper towel, for 5 to 6 minutes at HIGH (100%), until no longer pink, stirring twice. Drain well. Stir in hash browns.
3. Combine bread crumbs, ¾ cup shredded cheese, salt, pepper, and eggs in a bowl. Stir into sausage and hash browns. Microwave for 12 to 13 minutes at MEDIUM (50%), stirring twice. Sprinkle with remaining cheese; let stand 5 minutes. Cut into wedges and serve garnished with a tomato slice or sprig of fresh parsley, if desired.

Yield: 4 servings.

TIPS

For tips on how to make your own dry bread crumbs, see page 56.

You can substitute 1½ cups shredded cooked potatoes for the frozen hash browns. Then omit step #1.

For a Quick Quiche Lorraine: Omit broccoli. Microwave zucchini and onion for 2½ to 3 minutes at HIGH (100%) in step #1. Proceed as directed, stirring in ½-pound cooked crumbled bacon with the Swiss cheese.

1 cup chopped broccoli
½ cup thinly sliced zucchini
½ cup chopped green onion
4-ounce can mushrooms, drained
1½ cups (6 ounces) shredded Cheddar cheese, divided
1 cup (4 ounces) shredded Swiss cheese

1 cup milk
3 medium eggs
½ cup buttermilk baking mix
1 teaspoon Italian seasoning
1 teaspoon chopped chives or parsley
1 tomato or green pepper, to garnish

1. Butter a 10-inch microwave-safe glass pie plate. Combine broccoli, zucchini, and onion in pie plate. Cover with plastic wrap; microwave 4 to 5 minutes at HIGH (100%). Drain off excess liquid. Stir in mushrooms, 1 cup Cheddar cheese, and Swiss cheese.

2. Using a blender or electric mixer, beat milk, eggs, baking mix, seasoning, and chives until blended well. Pour over vegetables; microwave for 15 to 16 minutes at MEDIUM HIGH (70%), until center is almost set, rotating the plate twice. Sprinkle with the remaining ½ cup Cheddar cheese. Microwave for 1 minute longer at MEDIUM HIGH (70%). Let stand for 5 minutes. Garnish with tomato slices or green pepper slices.

Yield: 6 to 8 servings.

LASAGNA BRUNCH PIE

¼ cup chopped onion

1 pound lean ground beef, crumbled

1½ teaspoons Italian seasoning

6-ounce can tomato paste

1 cup shredded mozzarella cheese, divided

½ cup small-curd creamed cottage cheese, slightly drained

¼ cup grated Parmesan or Romano cheese

1 cup milk

½ cup buttermilk baking mix

2 medium eggs or 1 large egg

1 teaspoon seasoned salt (optional)

1 red or green pepper, to garnish

TIPS

If you like the taste of lasagna, you'll love Lasagna Brunch Pie!

1. Microwave onion and ground beef in a microwave-safe casserole dish, covered with a paper towel, for 4 to 5 minutes at HIGH (100%), or until meat is no longer pink. Drain off fat. Stir in seasoning, tomato paste, ½ cup mozzarella cheese, cottage cheese, and Parmesan cheese. Spoon mixture into a greased 10-inch microwave-safe pie plate.

2. Using a blender or electric mixer, beat milk, baking mix, eggs, and seasoned salt until blended well. Pour over hamburger mixture in plate. Prick hamburger mixture with a fork to allow the milk mixture to sink to the bottom. Microwave for 15 to 16 minutes at MEDIUM HIGH (70%), until center is almost set, rotating plate twice. Sprinkle with remaining ½ cup mozzarella cheese. Microwave 1 minute longer at MEDIUM HIGH (70%). Let stand 5 minutes. Garnish with red and green pepper slices, if desired.

Yield: 6 to 8 servings.

HOLIDAY SIDE DISHES AND ACCOMPANI-MENTS

· ❊ ·

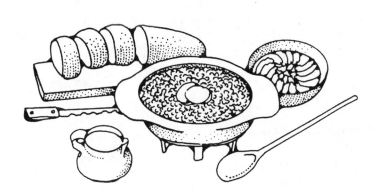

EASY AU GRATIN POTATOES

· · · · ·

A nice compliment to ham or roast beef.

1½ pounds (24 ounces)
   frozen hash browns
   (with onions and/or
   green pepper, optional)
8-ounce carton sour cream
1 can cream of potato
   soup, undiluted

1 to 2 cups (4 to 8 ounces)
   grated Cheddar cheese
   (either sharp or mild)
Dash of salt or pepper
2 tablespoons butter or
   margarine
Paprika (optional)

TIPS

If you like an extra-cheesy flavor, use 2 cups sharp Cheddar cheese instead of 1 cup.

1. Microwave frozen potatoes in a 2-quart covered microwave-safe casserole for 5 minutes at HIGH (100%). Stir in sour cream, soup, cheese, salt, and pepper. Dot with butter.
2. Microwave, covered, for 10 minutes at HIGH (100%). Stir. Sprinkle with paprika, if desired.
3. Microwave, covered, again for 10 to 12 minutes at MEDIUM (50%).* Let stand 5 minutes.

Yield: 4 servings.

---------- · ❄ · ----------

MASHED POTATOES IN ADVANCE
· · · · ·

Make these up to a day ahead of time. Refrigerate and then just heat and serve.

5–6 medium potatoes
 (about 2–2½ pounds),
 peeled and quartered
½ cup hot water
2 tablespoons butter or
 margarine
¼ cup milk

3-ounce package cream
 cheese, softened
¾ cup sour cream
1 tablespoon chopped
 chives
½ teaspoon garlic salt
1 teaspoon paprika

1. Microwave potatoes and water in a 2-quart flat casserole, covered, for 12 to 14 minutes at HIGH (100%), or until fork tender, stirring once. Drain.
2. Mash potatoes with butter using an electric mixer at low speed or a potato masher. Beat in milk, cream cheese, sour cream, chives, and garlic salt. Spread into a microwave-safe serving/casserole dish. Cover and refrigerate until just before serving time.

· ·
*Compacts: Microwave for 10 minutes at HIGH (100%) in step #3.
· ·
The fact that silence is golden may explain why there is so little of it.

TIPS
· · · · · · · ·

To ensure even cooking, use a flat casserole dish so the water covers the potatoes. Be sure to stir once halfway through the cooking time.

You can substitute ½ cup half-and-half for the milk, cream cheese, and sour cream in step #2.

3. Microwave, covered, for 8 to 10 minutes at MEDIUM HIGH (70%), until heated. Serve garnished with a sprinkle of paprika and 3 or 4 slices of butter, if desired.

Yield: 6 to 8 servings.

———— · ❄ · ————

TIPS
········
Half the recipe for a 1-pound squash: Microwave for 3 minutes at HIGH (100%) in step #1. Microwave for 5 to 6 minutes at HIGH (100%) in step #4.

I like to use Granny Smith or Golden Delicious apples because they lend a unique and delicious flavor to the squash.

APPLE-FILLED SQUASH
———— · · · · · ————

2 small or 1 large acorn squash (2 pounds)
½ cup brown sugar, packed
3 tablespoons butter or margarine, softened

½ teaspoon cinnamon
1 large apple, peeled, cored, and thinly sliced

1. Prick squash with a fork a few times to allow steam to escape while cooking. Microwave whole squash on a paper towel for 7 to 8 minutes at HIGH (100%). (Turn squash over halfway through cooking time to ensure even cooking.) Let stand 5 minutes.
2. Cut each partially cooked squash in half and scoop out seeds. Place in a microwave-safe casserole or serving plate.
3. Combine sugar, butter, cinnamon, and apple slices. Fill squash cavities. Cover with waxed paper.
4. Microwave 7 to 8 minutes at HIGH (100%), until apples and squash are tender. Let stand 5 minutes. Serve garnished with a dot of butter and a sprinkle of cinnamon.

Yield: 4 servings.

———— · ❄ · ————

SWEET POTATO BAKE

5–6 large sweet potatoes
   (3 pounds)
½ stick (¼ cup) butter or
  margarine, softened
8¼-ounce can crushed
  pineapple, drained
½ teaspoon cinnamon

¼ teaspoon nutmeg
Dash of salt
1½ cups miniature or 16
  large marshmallows
½ cup (2 ounces) chopped
  walnuts or pecans
  (optional)

1. Wash sweet potatoes. Prick skins with a fork. Microwave them on a paper towel, 1 inch apart, for 18 to 22 minutes at HIGH (100%). Let stand 10 minutes, covered with foil or a casserole dish, to soften.
2. Scoop out centers of potatoes into a 2-quart bowl. Discard skins. With an electric mixer, mash potatoes, 3 tablespoons butter, cinnamon, nutmeg, and salt until smooth. Gradually add pineapple and beat until fluffy. Stir in 1 cup marshmallows and ¼ cup nuts, if desired. Spoon into a buttered 2-quart microwave-safe casserole.
3. Microwave for 9 to 11 minutes at MEDIUM HIGH (70%).
4. Combine 1 tablespoon butter, ½ cup marshmallows, and ¼ cup nuts, if desired. Spread over cooked sweet potatoes. Let stand for 5 minutes until marshmallows are melted. Serve immediately.

Yield: 10 servings.

TIPS

Potatoes will *not* feel soft until after standing time in step #1.

Be sure to prick skins of sweet potatoes with a fork before microwaving so the buildup of steam doesn't cause them to explode in your microwave.

Variation: You can substitute a 32-ounce can yams or sweet potatoes, drained well, for the 5 large sweet potatoes. Microwave for 5 minutes at HIGH (100%) in a 2-quart bowl. Omit step #1. Proceed to beat with an electric mixer in step #2.

This is a beautiful and quick side dish to accompany any holiday entree.

Weigh your squash when you buy it. Whole squash requires 6 to 7 minutes per pound of cooking time. When done, it will be tender or soft when pricked with a fork.

ACORN SQUASH WITH CRANBERRY FILLING
—————— • • • • • ——————

1 tablespoon brown sugar, honey, or sugar substitute equivalent
16-ounce can jellied or whole cranberry sauce

1 large (2 pounds) acorn squash or 2 small acorn squash

1. Combine brown sugar and cranberry sauce. Microwave for 2 minutes at HIGH (100%). Set aside.
2. Prick squash to allow steam to escape.
3. Microwave whole squash on a paper towel or napkin for 12 to 14 minutes at HIGH (100%), until tender, turning over halfway through cooking time.
4. Let stand 2 minutes.
5. Cut into halves or quarters. Remove seeds.
6. Fill with cranberry sauce mixture and microwave again for 2 minutes at HIGH (100%) to heat through.

Yield: 2 to 4 servings.

———————— · ❄ · ————————

SWEET CREAMED VEGETABLE MEDLEY
—————— • • • • ——————

1 pound (16 ounces) frozen mixed vegetables: carrots, broccoli, cauliflower, and zucchini
⅓ cup butter or margarine
2 tablespoons cornstarch
2 tablespoons nondairy creamer

1 cup milk
1 cup (4 ounces) grated Swiss cheese
Dash of salt and pepper
2 tablespoons grated Parmesan cheese to garnish

You can use any frozen vegetables in this recipe.

1. Place frozen mixed vegetables in a 1-quart microwave-safe casserole. Cover with casserole lid. Microwave for 7 to 8 minutes at HIGH (100%), or until tender. Let stand 5 minutes while making sauce.

2. Microwave butter in a 1-quart microwave-safe bowl for 30 to 40 seconds at HIGH (100%) to melt. Blend in cornstarch and creamer. Stir in milk until smooth. Microwave for 3 to 4 minutes at HIGH (100%) or until thickened, stirring twice. Stir in Swiss cheese and seasoning, stirring until cheese is melted.

3. Pour sauce over vegetables. Toss to coat all vegetables. Microwave for 3 to 4 minutes at HIGH (100%), or until sauce is bubbly. Serve garnished with grated Parmesan cheese.

Yield: 4 to 6 servings.

. ❄ .

CHRISTMAS FRUIT SALAD

16-ounce can juice-packed fruit cocktail

¾ cup milk

3½-ounce package pistachio nut pudding mix (not instant)

1½ cups (3½ ounces) whipped topping

1 apple, cored and sliced

1 cup grapes (seedless or seeds removed)

2 cups frozen bing cherries

11-ounce can mandarin oranges (or 1 cup sliced, fresh orange), drained

1 cup miniature or 11 large marshmallows (optional)

TIPS

Fruit juice plus milk should equal 1½ cups liquid in step #1. If there is not enough juice, add water to milk and juice to make 1½ cups.

1. Drain juice from fruit cocktail in a 2-quart microwave bowl. Set fruit aside. Stir milk into juice. Add pudding mix and stir well.

2. Microwave for 5½ to 6½ minutes at HIGH (100%),* or until boiling, stirring once. Chill ½ hour.

*Compacts: Microwave for 7 to 8 minutes at HIGH (100%), until boiling.

3. Fold whipped topping into pudding mixture. Add fruit and marshmallows (if desired). Cover and refrigerate 1 to 2 hours before serving.

Yield: 6 to 8 servings.

———————— · ❄ · ————————

. . . .

Variation: Coconut Christmas Fruit Salad: Substitute 1 package coconut cream pudding mix for the pistachio nut pudding mix.

CANDIED CINNAMON APPLE CHUNKS OR RINGS

———————— · · · · · ————————

1 cup hot water	6 medium apples, peeled,
½ cup sugar	cored, and cut into 1-
½ cup (4 ounces) red-hot	inch chunks or ½-inch
cinnamon candies	rings (about 2 pounds)

1. Combine water, sugar, and candies in a 2-quart microwave-safe bowl. Microwave, uncovered, for 6 to 8 minutes at HIGH (100%), or until almost all of the candies are dissolved, stirring once. Remove any uncooked candy from syrup.
2. Add prepared apples to candy syrup, stirring to coat all of the apple pieces. Cover with waxed paper. Microwave for 9 to 10 minutes at HIGH (100%), or until apples are tender. Let stand 5 minutes. Serve as a garnish/accompaniment with pork or poultry, or cool at least 3 hours and serve as a dessert or side dish with any meal.

Yield: 4 to 6 servings.

———————— · ❄ · ————————

T I P S
. . . .

Jonathan or Gravenstein apples make especially delicious candied apples.

After 3 hours in the refrigerator the apple syrup will thicken.

If you like a strong cinnamon flavor, increase the cinnamon candies to ⅔ cup.

EASY TWO-LAYER CHERRY GELATIN MOLD

— — — — · · · · · — — — —

1¾ cups water

6-ounce package cherry (or any other flavor) gelatin, dry

16-ounce can juice-packed fruit cocktail

Cold water

4 ounces cream cheese (½ of 8-ounce package)

Parsley sprig plus fruit to garnish, optional

1. Microwave water in a 2-quart microwave-safe bowl for 3 to 3½ minutes at HIGH (100%), or until boiling. Dissolve gelatin in boiling water. Stir well.

2. Drain fruit cocktail, reserving juice. Set fruit aside. Pour juice into a 1-cup measure. Add enough cold water to the juice to make 1 cup. Pour into the dissolved gelatin. Mix well. Measure out 1 cup gelatin. Chill remaining gelatin until thickened (about 1 hour).

3. Microwave cream cheese, unwrapped, in a small microwave-safe bowl for 30 to 40 seconds at HIGH (100%). Stir into 1 cup of gelatin until smooth. Set aside.

4. Add fruit cocktail to chilled, thickened gelatin and pour into a 5- or 6-cup lightly greased mold, bowl, or loaf pan or 8 to 10 individual molds. Chill about 10 minutes. Top with gelatin–cream cheese mixture. Chill until firm, about 2 to 3 hours. Unmold onto lettuce or endive leaves. Serve garnished with a parsley sprig and a cherry or other fruit.

Yield: 8 to 10 servings.

— — — — · ❄ · — — — —

TIPS
·······

Add ½ cup additional fresh fruits or nuts to the chilled gelatin with the fruit cocktail in step #4.

For a large batch of cranberry sauce: Double ingredients; use a 3-quart casserole. Microwave for 6 minutes in step #2 and for 8 to 10 minutes in step #3.

For Cranapple Sauce: Add 1 small cored, peeled, and grated apple to the cranberries in step #1. Increase microwaving time by 1 minute in step #3. Strain and refrigerate.

For Cranberry and Orange Relish: Substitute 1 small seeded and chopped orange for the water (use a food processor to chop orange, if available). Proceed as directed for Cranberry Sauce, but lower power setting to MEDIUM (50%) in step #3.

Omit bacon and step #1, if desired. Serve chowder garnished with chopped fresh parsley.

CRANBERRY SAUCE

So easy to prepare before a holiday meal.

2 cups fresh cranberries (½ pound), washed

1 cup sugar
½ cup water

1. Combine all ingredients in a 1-quart microwave-safe casserole. Cover with waxed paper.
2. Microwave for 3 minutes at HIGH (100%). Stir.
3. Cover again. Microwave again for 4 to 5 minutes at HIGH (100%),* until the skins pop. Strain if desired.
4. Pour into serving container. Refrigerate to thicken.

Yield: 8 servings.

QUICK CLAM CHOWDER

3 slices bacon
6½- or 7½-ounce can minced clams, drained, reserving juice
2 medium potatoes, cut into ½-inch cubes (1½ cups)
2 tablespoons diced onion
1 can cream of celery soup, undiluted

1½ cups milk
½ teaspoon seasoned pepper (optional)
1 tablespoon fresh parsley, chopped, or 1 teaspoon dried parsley

1. Microwave bacon in a 2-quart microwave-safe casserole, between four layers of paper towels, for 3 to 4 minutes at HIGH (100%), until crisp. Remove bacon; set aside. Discard paper towels and grease.

*Compacts: Microwave for 6 to 7 minutes at HIGH (100%).

2. Combine reserved clam juice, cubed potatoes, and onion in a microwave-safe casserole. Cover. Microwave 10 to 12 minutes at HIGH (100%), until vegetables are tender.

3. Stir in soup, milk, pepper, and parsley. Microwave, uncovered, 7 to 9 minutes at HIGH (100%), until mixture almost boils, stirring three times. (*Do not boil.*)

4. Stir in clams. Microwave 1 to 2 minutes at HIGH (100%) to heat. Crumble bacon and sprinkle over chowder just before serving.

Yield: 5 to 6 servings.

---- · ❄ · ----

Variation: Creamy Clam Chowder: Omit cream of celery soup and milk. Add ¼ cup chopped celery in step #2. Add 2½ cups half-and-half or evaporated milk in step #3. Proceed as directed.

QUICK POTATO SALAD

5 to 6 medium potatoes, peeled and cubed (2 to 2½ pounds)
½ cup water
4 large eggs
¼ cup minced celery (optional)
¼ cup minced onion
Salt and pepper, to taste

1 cup mayonnaise, mixed with 2 tablespoons milk
2 teaspoons dry mustard
2 teaspoons sugar or sweetener (optional)
1 tablespoon vinegar
Paprika plus chopped parsley to garnish (optional)

1. Microwave potatoes and water in a 2-quart flat casserole, covered, for 12 to 14 minutes at HIGH (100%) until tender, stirring once. Drain. Set aside to cool.

2. Break eggs into four custard cups. Prick yolks twice with a fork. Cover with waxed paper. Microwave for 3 to 4 minutes at MEDIUM (50%), until white is set and yolk

You can use 8 to 10 ounces of fresh minced clams instead of the 6½-ounce can: Microwave fresh clams in a small casserole with ⅓ cup water for 4 to 5 minutes at HIGH (100%) until clams are set. Use liquid and clams to replace can of clams.

Variation: 32 ounces
frozen Southern-style
hash browns can be
substituted for fresh po-
tatoes. Omit water. Mi-
crowave as directed in
step #1.

is almost set, rotating each cup once for even cooking. Let stand 1 minute to complete cooking. Cool and chop coarsely.

3. About 2 to 3 hours before serving, mix celery, onion, seasonings, and eggs with potatoes in a serving dish. Combine mayonnaise and milk, mustard, sugar, and vinegar in a small bowl; stir into vegetables. Garnish with paprika and parsley, if desired. Refrigerate until serving time to blend flavors.

Yield: 8 to 10 servings.

--- · ❄ · ---

TIPS
·······

This coleslaw will stay
crisp and fresh in your
refrigerator for a week.

PICNIC COLESLAW

--- · · · · · ---

Avoid the rush! Make this recipe the day before and refrigerate overnight.

1 large head cabbage, shredded	1 cup sugar
1 medium onion, diced (optional)	1 cup white vinegar
	½ cup vegetable oil
2 carrots, shredded	1 teaspoon dry mustard
	2 teaspoons celery seed

1. Combine prepared vegetables in a large bowl or crock; set aside.
2. Combine remaining ingredients in a 1-quart microwave-safe bowl. Microwave for 2½ to 3 minutes at HIGH (100%), until boiling. Stir until smooth. Cool completely.
3. Pour over vegetables. Cover tightly and refrigerate at least 2 hours or overnight.

Yield: 12 to 16 servings.

--- · ❄ · ---

·······································

The work will wait while you show a child a rainbow. The rainbow won't wait while you do the work.

EASY PICNIC BAKED BEANS

2 16-ounce cans pork and
beans
¼ cup brown sugar,
packed
½ cup ketchup

1 tablespoon dry mustard
6 slices bacon, cut into 1-
inch strips

1. Place 1 can of beans in a 1-quart microwave-safe casserole. Combine sugar, ketchup, and mustard; spread half of mixture on beans. Add remaining can of beans. Top with ketchup sauce. Microwave for 3 minutes at HIGH (100%). Stir slightly.
2. Place bacon slices on top of heated casserole. Microwave again, for 11 to 12 minutes at MEDIUM HIGH (70%), covered with waxed paper. Let stand 5 minutes.

Yield: 8 to 10 servings.

GREEN BEANS ALMONDINE

½ clove garlic, minced
2 tablespoons butter or
margarine, divided
1 pound fresh green
beans, ends removed,
cut into 1½-inch pieces

2 tablespoons water
¼ cup toasted slivered
almonds
Salt and pepper, to taste
1 tablespoon butter

1. Combine garlic and 1 tablespoon butter in a 1-quart microwave-safe casserole. Microwave, covered, for 1 minute at HIGH (100%).
2. Stir in prepared beans and water. Cover tightly. Microwave for 9 to 11 minutes at HIGH (100%), or until beans are tender, stirring twice. Drain slightly.

For sweeter baked beans, increase brown sugar from ¼ cup to ½ cup.

You can substitute ½ cup sliced water chestnuts, drained, for the slivered almonds.

To toast almonds (or water chestnuts): Microwave 1 teaspoon butter with ¼ cup almonds (or water chestnuts) on a pie plate for 2 to 2½ minutes at HIGH (100%), stirring frequently, until evenly browned. (Water chestnuts may need 1 additional minute of microwaving time. They will not look very brown.)

3. Stir in toasted almonds and seasonings. Top with 1 tablespoon butter and serve.

Yield: 4 to 6 servings.

———————— · ❄ · ————————

CAESAR-STYLE GREEN BEANS
· · · · ·

1 pound fresh green
   beans, prepared and cut
   into 2-inch pieces
   (3 cups)
2 tablespoons diced onion
1 clove garlic, crushed, or
   ⅛ teaspoon garlic
   powder
¼ cup water
1 tablespoon cider or
   white vinegar
1 tablespoon vegetable oil

Dash of salt and pepper,
   optional
2 tablespoons dry bread
   crumbs
2 tablespoons grated
   Parmesan cheese
2 teaspoons butter or
   margarine
Paprika or microwave
   browning powder for
   chicken (optional)

1. Microwave green beans, onion, garlic, and water in a 1½-quart microwave-safe casserole, covered, for 9 to 11 minues at HIGH (100%), stirring once. Drain.
2. Combine vinegar, oil, and seasonings with beans in the casserole. Mix bread crumbs, cheese and butter; sprinkle over beans. Sprinkle with paprika or browning powder. Microwave for 2 to 3 minutes at HIGH (100%), until heated.

Yield: 4 servings.

———————— · ❄ · ————————

Those who sow courtesy reap friendship, and those who plant kindness gather love.

HARVEST-TIME ZUCCHINI

4 cups sliced (1½ pounds) zucchini, ¼–½-inch thick (washed but not pared)

2 tablespoons butter or margarine

½ cup diced onion

½ cup dairy sour cream

2 tablespoons milk

1 teaspoon seasoned salt or salt

1 teaspoon paprika

1 teaspoon poppy seed

1. In a 1½-quart microwave-safe casserole, combine zucchini, butter, and onion. Microwave, covered, for 6 to 7 minutes at HIGH (100%), or until tender, stirring once.
2. Mix remaining ingredients; gently stir into zucchini. Microwave for 2 to 3 minutes at MEDIUM HIGH (70%), until heated.

Yield: 4 servings.

* * *

ZUCCHINI-TOMATO CASSEROLE

1 pound ground beef, crumbled

1 teaspoon microwave browning powder for meat, garlic and onion flavored (optional)

⅓ cup chopped onion

Dash of seasoned salt

5 cups (1¾ pounds) sliced zucchini (¼-inch slices)

16-ounce can stewed tomatoes

2 cups (8 ounces) shredded mozzarella or Monterey Jack cheese

1. Combine ground beef, browning powder (optional), and onion in a microwave-safe dish. Microwave for 5 minutes at HIGH (100%), covered with a paper towel, and stirring once. Drain. Add seasoned salt. Set aside.

TIPS

For a meatless casserole: Omit ground beef, browning powder, and onions, as well as step #1. Proceed as directed, omitting meat layer in step #3.

2. Microwave zucchini in a 2-quart microwave-safe casserole, covered, for 7 to 8 minutes at HIGH (100%), stirring once.

3. Remove half the zucchini from the casserole. Layer half the meat, tomatoes, and cheese on top of the zucchini. Repeat layers. Cover with waxed paper. Microwave for 4 to 5 minutes at MEDIUM HIGH (70%), or until cheese is melted. Let stand 2 to 3 minutes.

Yield: 4 to 6 servings.

———————— · ❄ · ————————

HOLIDAY MEATS AND MAIN DISHES

· ❄ ·

STANDING RIB ROAST WITH AU JUS SAUCE

· · · · ·

For New Years Day or Father's Day

1 standing rib roast (3 to 8
   pounds), small end*
3 cloves garlic, peeled and
   pressed or processed in
   a food processor to
   make a paste

*You can substitute a rolled rib roast for the standing rib roast.

TIPS

A microwaved stand-
ing rib roast is often
more tender than a
conventionally roasted
one and a lot quicker
to cook.

Allow ¾ pound bone-
in or ½ pound bone-
less roast per person.

Do not salt the roast
during microwaving, as
salt toughens the meat.

Shield any pointed edges with 1-inch strips of foil (see shielding tips, page 9) before step #3.

A temperature probe will help determine doneness. Insert it into the center of the meat (away from the bone, fat, or foil) after turning roast over in step #4. Set oven for internal temperature listed next to desired doneness (see chart) and microwave at MEDIUM (50%). Let stand as directed.

1. Carefully cut fat from roast so it can be folded back, but is still attached at one end. Turn back fat and rub garlic paste over roast. Cover garlic paste and roast with fat.
2. Place roast on roasting rack fat side up. Cover or tent with folded waxed paper. Microwave for 6 to 8 minutes at HIGH (100%).
3. Turn roast over. Cover again. Microwave for half of the calculated microwaving time at MEDIUM (50%) (see chart below).
4. Turn roast fat side up again. Cover again. Microwave for remainder of cooking time at MEDIUM (50%), or to desired internal temperature/doneness. Cover with foil, and let stand on kitchen counter for 10 to 15 minutes. Season with salt, if desired. Slice and serve immediately with Au Jus Sauce.

STANDING RIB ROAST OR ROLLED ROAST MICROWAVING CHART

Desired Doneness	Minutes per pound at MEDIUM (50%)	Internal Temperature
Rare	10–13 min. lb.	120° F.
Medium	13–15 min. lb.	135° F.
Well Done	15–17 min. lb.	150° F.

AU JUS SAUCE

· · · · ·

¾ ounce package Au Jus Mix
1 cup water

½ cup dry red wine
Drippings from roast, fat removed (about ½ cup)

1. Combine all ingredients in a 1-quart microwave-safe bowl until blended. Microwave for 3 to 4 minutes at HIGH (100%), or until thickened.

TURKEY BREAST FOR MOTHER'S DAY

——————— • • • • • ———————

Turkey for a small crowd.

2½ –4-pound turkey
  breast
2 tablespoons vegetable oil
  or margarine

Poultry seasoning
Paprika or browning
  powder

1. Rinse and dry defrosted turkey breast. Brush breast with oil and sprinkle liberally with poultry seasoning and paprika or browning powder. Place, skin side down, on a microwave roasting/bacon rack. Cover loosely with plastic wrap.
2. Calculate total cooking time allowing 14 to 16 minutes per pound. Divide time in half. Microwave for 5 minutes at HIGH (100%). Reduce power to MEDIUM (50%) and microwave remainder of first half of time.
3. Turn skin side up. Baste and season as in step #1. Microwave for last half of total time at MEDIUM (50%), or until a probe inserted in the meatiest area registers 170°F. Let stand on kitchen counter 10 to 15 minutes tented with foil. Garnish, if desired, with sugared grapes (dip small clusters of green grapes first in egg white and then in sugar) to garnish (optional) or fresh parsley.

To defrost frozen turkey breast: Microwave for 4 minutes per pound at DEFROST (30%). Let stand 30 minutes to allow the inside of the turkey to continue to defrost.

To cook turkey in a microwave cooking plastic bag: Prepare as directed in step #1. Place in bag that has been

TIPS
········

Before cooking in the microwave oven, always defrost the turkey breast, remove excess fat or tail piece, rinse, and pat dry with a paper towel.

The pop-out timer that comes with some turkey breasts usually will not pop out during the microwaving time. It may pop out during the standing time.

Microwave-safe plastic cooking bags help ensure even cooking for turkey breasts. Instead of pricking holes in the bag as the manufacturer often recommends, when tying the bag leave a ½-inch opening for the air vent. This will help prevent the liquid and fat from spilling out when the breast is turned over.

dusted with 1 tablespoon flour. Fasten with plastic tie or string, leaving a ½-inch opening. Microwave for 12 to 15 minutes per pound at MEDIUM (50%). Let stand on kitchen counter 20 minutes in bag.

Yield: 6 to 8 servings.

———————— · ❄ · ————————

OVEN-ROASTED TURKEY

———————— · · · · · ————————

10–22-pound turkey
½ stick (¼ cup) margarine
  (soft or melted) or
  vegetable oil

Poultry seasoning
Paprika or browning
  powder

1. Rinse and dry defrosted turkey. Stuff if desired. Tie legs together. Brush entire bird with margarine and sprinkle liberally with poultry seasoning and paprika or browning powder. Place turkey breast side down on a roasting rack. Shield turkey legs and wings with aluminum foil. Cover loosely with a piece of folded (tented) waxed paper. (Or place in a plastic cooking bag that has been dusted on the inside with 1 tablespoon of flour [see Tip]).
2. Calculate total cooking time allowing 9 to 12 minutes per pound.* Divide time in half. Microwave at HIGH (100%)† 10 minutes. Reduce power to MEDIUM HIGH (70%) and microwave remainder of first half of total time. Remove excess liquid and fat from roasting rack.
3. Turn turkey breast side up; baste. Microwave at MEDIUM HIGH for last half of total time, or until probe registers 175°F. in the white meat. Let stand 15 minutes

....

*If turkey is stuffed: Add 1 pound to the weight of the turkey when calculating total cooking time.
†Compacts: Follow the same directions using a small turkey (8–10-pound) turkey and allowing 8 minutes per pound at HIGH (100%) in steps #2 and #3.

TIPS
········

Always defrost the turkey, remove the giblets and neck, rinse, and pat it dry with a paper towel before cooking it in the microwave oven.

I have cooked up to a 22-pound turkey in the microwave oven. However, a 12- to 14-pound turkey works best.

My favorite way to cook turkey is in a plastic cooking bag: Tie the legs together with a string or dental floss. Brush the bird with margarine and sprinkle with seasoning and browning powder. Shield the wings and legs. Place bird in the plastic cooking bag that has been dusted with 1 tablespoon flour. Tie the bag shut in oven or on kitchen counter tented with foil or a kitchen towel.

To defrost frozen turkey: Microwave for 4 minutes per pound at DEFROST (30%). (For best results, allow turkey to stand for 15 minutes halfway through defrosting time and turn turkey over three to four times while defrosting.) Let turkey stand on kitchen counter for 60 minutes to complete defrosting before cooking it.

Yield: Figure 1 serving per pound.

———————— · ❄ · ————————

Variation: Combination Method (to speed conventional oven baking and browning): Prepare as directed above in step #1. Place in a plastic cooking bag, as directed (see Tip). Microwave for 1 hour at MEDIUM HIGH (70%), turning over once. Transfer to a conventional oven (preheated to 350°F.); bake for 1 to 1½ hours. Let stand as directed in step #3.

Variation: For Convection Microwave: Prepare as directed in step #1. Place in a plastic cooking bag, as directed (see Tip). High Mix Bake at 375°F. (or Combination #2 or Code #2 at 375°F.) for 7 to 9 minutes per pound. Let stand as directed in step #3.

with the plastic tie, string, or dental floss, leaving a ½-inch opening for an air vent. Place bag of turkey on a bacon rack or in a flat casserole dish. Proceed with step #2.

See page 9 for shielding instructions.

The pop-out timer that comes with some turkeys will not work properly in a microwave oven. The turkey will be cooked before the timer pops out. It may pop out during standing time.

Serve as a side dish anytime or use for stuffing the bird.

1 cup diced celery
1 stick (½ cup) butter or
  margarine
1 cup diced onion
¼ teaspoon pepper
2 teaspoons poultry
  seasoning or sage
1 tablespoon minced fresh
  parsley or 1 teaspoon
  parsley flakes

2 teaspoons chicken
  bouillon granules (or 2
  cubes), dissolved in ¾
  cup hot water
1 egg, beaten (optional)
8 cups dry bread cubes or
  seasoned stuffing mix

TIPS

The egg can be omitted, if desired, but it does make moister and firmer stuffing.

If you use seasoned stuffing mix, reduce poultry seasoning by 1 teaspoon.

To make your own dry bread cubes, leave bread uncovered for a day, or see page 56.

1. Microwave celery, onion, and butter in a covered 2-quart microwave-safe casserole for 4 to 5 minutes at HIGH (100%), until vegetables are tender.
2. Stir in seasonings, bouillon, and egg (optional). Add bread cubes and toss with a fork to mix.
3. **To serve:** Microwave, covered, for 6 to 7 minutes at MEDIUM HIGH (70%), until hot, stirring twice. Fluff with a fork. Serve as a side dish with any poultry or meat.

To stuff poultry: Stuff a 12- to 15-pound turkey (or 3 chickens) and bake as usual or microwave (see page 229).

Yield: 8 to 10 servings, or stuffing for 12- to 15-pound turkey.

Variations: You can add any of the following to the stuffing recipe:
  1 cup giblets, cooked and chopped
  ½ cup raisins and ½ cup chopped walnuts or pecans
  4-ounce can sliced mushrooms, not drained
  ½ cup slivered almonds

APRICOT AND PECAN GLAZED HAM

————— · · · · · —————

2½–4-pound boneless,
  cooked ham
1 teaspoon water
1 teaspoon dry mustard

½ cup apricot preserves
¼ cup chopped pecans
Dash of ground cinnamon
Dash of ground cloves

1. Place ham, fat side down, on a microwave roasting rack. Cover loosely with plastic wrap. Microwave for 10 to 12 minutes at HIGH (100%). Turn ham over. Microwave again, covered, 7 to 9 minutes per pound at MEDIUM (50%).
2. Mix water with mustard; combine with preserves, pecans, cinnamon, and cloves. Spread over ham. Cover again with plastic wrap. Microwave for 6 to 8 minutes at MEDIUM (50%), (or to 130°F.). Cover with foil and let stand on kitchen counter 10 minutes.

Yield: 10 to 16 servings.

————— · ❄ · —————

HOLIDAY GLAZED HAM FOR NEW YEAR'S DAY

————— · · · · · —————

················· PINEAPPLE GLAZE ··················

8-ounce can crushed
  pineapple
⅔ cup brown sugar,
  packed

2 teaspoons prepared
  mustard
½ teaspoon dry mustard

TIPS
········

For a 1-pound ham slice: Choose and prepare one-half any of the glaze recipes. Microwave ham slice, covered with plastic wrap, on a roasting rack for 6 to 8 minutes at MEDIUM HIGH (70%). Cover with glaze. Microwave for 1 to 2 minutes longer at MEDIUM HIGH (70%).

If top edge of ham begins to overcook, shield it with 1½-inch strip of foil (see page 9 for tips on shielding).

TIPS
········

To microwave a 2½ to 5-pound *uncooked fresh ham:* Place ham in a microwave-safe plastic cooking bag. Tie bag shut, leaving a ½-inch opening for an air vent. Place on a roasting rack. Microwave for 15 minutes at HIGH (100%). Turn ham over. Microwave again for 15 to 18 minutes per pound at MEDIUM (50%), or until well done (or about 160°F.), spreading with one of the glazes for the last 5 minutes of cooking time. Let stand on kitchen counter in bag 10 to 15 minutes.

If you are using a temperature probe, insert it into the center of the ham after spreading the glaze on it in step #3. Program it for 130°F. at MEDIUM (50%).

If top edge of ham begins to overcook, shield it (see Tip, p. 9).

(see Tip, p. 9).

·················· HONEY-ORANGE GLAZE ··················

2 tablespoons orange juice (fresh squeezed is best)
¾ cup honey

¼ teaspoon cinnamon
¼ teaspoon ground cloves

·················· CHERRY GLAZE ··················

21-ounce can cherry pie filling
1 tablespoon lemon juice
¼ teaspoon ground cloves

2½ –4-pound boneless, cooked ham

1. Combine ingredients for the glaze of your choice. Set aside.
2. Place ham, fat side down, on a microwave roasting rack. Cover loosely with plastic wrap. Microwave for 10 to 12 minutes at HIGH (100%). Turn ham over. Cover with plastic wrap again.
3. Microwave again for 8 to 10 minutes per pound at MEDIUM (50%), (or to 130°F.),* spreading with half the glaze the last 5 minutes of cooking time.
4. Top with remaining glaze. Cover with aluminum foil and let stand on kitchen counter 10 minutes.

Yield: 10 to 12 servings.

———— · ❄ · ————

··

*Compacts: Microwave for 8 to 9 minutes per pound at HIGH (100%) in step #3.

VICTORIA DAY LEG OF LAMB
WITH SHERRY MUSHROOM
SAUCE OR MINT SAUCE

· · · · ·

4- –5-pound leg of lamb,
bone-in*

3 cloves garlic, peeled and
pressed or processed in
a food processor to
make a paste

1 teaspoon thyme

1 teaspoon rosemary

2 tablespoons vegetable or
olive oil

1. Cut several ½-inch slits in lamb. Rub garlic paste into
   each slit. Mix thyme, rosemary, and oil; rub mixture over
   entire surface of lamb.
2. Place lamb fat side down on a roasting rack. Cover or tent
   with waxed paper. Microwave for 6 to 8 minutes at
   HIGH (100%).
3. Reduce power to MEDIUM (50%). Microwave for half of
   the calculated microwaving time (see chart page 235).
4. Turn lamb fat side up. Cover again. Microwave for remainder of cooking time at MEDIUM (50%), or to desired internal temperature/doneness. Cover with foil, and
   let stand on kitchen counter for 10 minutes. Season with
   salt, if desired. Slice and serve immediately with Sherry
   Mushroom Sauce or Mint Sauce.

Yield: 4 to 6 servings.

———— · ❄ · ————

TIPS
········

To prevent narrow
bone end of leg from
overcooking, shield it
with a 2-inch strip of
foil (see shielding tips
on page 9) before mi-
crowaving in step #2.
Remove foil shielding
after turning lamb fat-
side up in step #4.

A rolled lamb roast
does not need shield-
ing.

To check doneness in
step #4, insert your mi-
crowave probe (see tips
for using probe, page
10) or microwave meat
thermometer into the
center of the meat but
not touching the bone
or fat.

*You can substitute a rolled lamb roast for the leg of lamb.

Desired Doneness	Minutes per pound at MEDIUM (50%)	Internal Temperature
Rare	9–12 min. lb.	120° F.
Medium	10–13 min. lb.	135° F.
Well Done	11–14 min. lb.	150° F.

SHERRY MUSHROOM SAUCE

. . . . .

2 tablespoons butter or
    margarine
1 tablespoon flour
4-ounce can sliced
    mushrooms, drained
    and liquid reserved
1 cup half-and-half

1 tablespoon sherry or
    white wine
½ teaspoon seasoned salt
¼ teaspoon each dried
    tarragon and rosemary

1. Microwave margarine in a 1-quart microwave-safe bowl
   for 30 to 40 seconds at HIGH (100%). Stir in flour; add
   liquid from mushrooms, half-and-half, and sherry. Stir in
   seasoned salt, tarragon, and rosemary until blended. Microwave for 3 to 3½ minutes at MEDIUM HIGH (70%),
   or until thickened. Stir in sliced mushrooms. Microwave
   for 1 minute longer at MEDIUM HIGH (70%) to heat
   mushrooms through.

MINT SAUCE

. . . . .

½ cup white vinegar
2 tablespoons water

¼ cup sugar
½ cup minced mint leaves

1. Combine vinegar, water, and sugar in a 2-cup glass measure. Microwave for 40 to 60 seconds at HIGH (100%) or
   until boiling. Add mint leaves and let stand at least one
   hour.

BARBEQUED SPARERIBS FOR CANADA DAY (OR INDEPENDENCE DAY)

····· ·····

·············· BARBEQUE SAUCE ·············

1 medium onion, finely
chopped
1 clove garlic, minced
(optional)
1 tablespoon vegetable oil
3 tablespoons brown
sugar, packed
3 tablespoons cider
vinegar

¾ cup catsup
1 teaspoon dry mustard
1 tablespoon
Worcestershire sauce
¼ cup tomato juice or
water

·············· RIBS ·············

3 to 4 pounds meaty
spareribs cut into 2-rib
pieces

1 cup water

1. **Sauce:** Combine onion, garlic, and oil in a 1-quart micro-wave-safe bowl. Microwave for 2½ to 3½ minutes at HIGH (100%) or until vegetables are tender. Mix in remaining ingredients. Microwave for 3 to 4 minutes at HIGH (100%) until thickened, stirring twice. Set aside.
2. **Ribs:** Arrange ribs in a single layer in a 12 × 8-inch microwave-safe baking dish with meatiest portions to the outside. Pour water over ribs. Cover with waxed paper. Microwave for 5 minutes at HIGH (100%). Rearrange ribs. Cover again. Microwave for 15 to 20 minutes at MEDIUM (50%), until partially cooked. Drain off all water and fat.
3. **To grill ribs:** Place drained ribs on a preheated gas or charcoal grill over a medium fire. Baste with prepared

You do not have to worry about your ribs burning on the grill before they are done if you follow this recipe, which partially cooks the ribs in the micro-wave oven first.

When purchasing ribs, figure ¾ pound of meaty spareribs per person.

When microwaving ribs, be sure to place the meatiest portions toward the outside of the dish and do not overlap them or the ribs will not cook evenly.

sauce often and turn over as needed. Grill 25 to 30 minutes.

To microwave ribs (instead of grilling): Pour sauce over drained ribs. Cover with waxed paper. Microwave for 20 to 30 minutes at MEDIUM (50%) or until fork tender, turning over and rearranging twice during microwave cooking time. Let stand 10 minutes.

Yield: 4 to 6 servings.

———————— · ❈ · ————————

Variation: For 8 to 10 servings of grilled Barbequed Ribs: Increase spareribs to 6 to 7 pounds. Microwave one-half of ribs at a time as directed in step #2. Use the same amount of Barbeque Sauce. Proceed as directed to grill ribs in step #3.

TIPS
....
Although this dinner takes more than an hour in the microwave oven, it still is a time savings over the conventional oven method that takes about 4 hours.

CORNED BEEF AND CABBAGE DINNER FOR ST. PATRICK'S DAY

——————— · · · · · ———————

2½ to 3 pounds corned beef brisket with seasoning packet
1 cup hot tap water
4 large carrots, peeled and sliced ½-inch thick

2 large potatoes, peeled and cut into chunks
1 medium head cabbage, rinsed and cut into wedges
1 large onion, cut into chunks

1. Place corned beef and the seasoning that comes with it in a 2- or 3-quart microwave-safe casserole. Add water. Cover with glass lid or plastic wrap (vent one edge). Microwave for 15 minutes at HIGH (100%).
2. Reduce power; microwave for 25 minutes at MEDIUM (50%). Turn meat over and add vegetables. Cover again.

3. Microwave for 55 to 60 minutes at MEDIUM (50%) or until meat is fork tender. Let stand 10 minutes.

Yield: 4 to 6 servings.

————————— · ❄ · —————————

Variation: For 8 to 10 servings: Increase corned beef to 5 pounds, carrots to 6, and potatoes to 3 or 4 large. Proceed as directed in steps #1 and #2. Microwave for 70 to 90 minutes in step #3.

PORK CHOPS AND YAM DINNER
————————— · · · · · —————————

4–6 (1-inch) boneless pork loins/chops (about 1½ pounds)

32-ounce can yams, drained (reserve ½ cup juice)

1 teaspoon lemon juice

1 tablespoon brown sugar, packed

6-ounce can frozen orange juice concentrate

Browning powder for meat

1½ tablespoons cornstarch dissolved in ¼ cup water

1. Place chops in a flat 10-inch microwave-safe casserole with the meatiest portions toward the outside. Combine yam juice, lemon juice, brown sugar, and orange juice concentrate. Pour over chops.
2. Cover with casserole lid. Microwave for 5 minutes at HIGH (100%). Sprinkle with browning powder. Cover again.
3. Microwave for 15 minutes at MEDIUM (50%). Turn chops over, sprinkle with browning powder, and microwave again for 10 to 15 minutes at MEDIUM (50%).
4. Add sliced yams. Microwave for 5 to 6 minutes at HIGH (100%). Drain liquid to a 1-quart microwave-safe bowl. Let chops and yams stand covered. Add cornstarch and

water to the drained liquid. Microwave for 3 to 4 minutes at HIGH (100%) to thicken. Serve sauce over pork chops and yams.

Yield: 4 to 6 servings.

————————— · ❉ · —————————

CHICKEN KIEV

————————— · · · · · —————————

Microwave easy!

1½-pound boneless chicken breasts (4–6 pieces)

4–6 tablespoons frozen butter, sliced

⅔ cup bread crumbs or cornflake crumbs

⅓ cup grated Parmesan cheese

½ teaspoon garlic salt

1 teaspoon paprika

1 tablespoon chopped parsley

3 tablespoons flour

1 medium egg, beaten

Browning powder for chicken (optional)

1. Pound chicken breasts flat with a mallet or side of a saucer until ¼-inch thick. Place 1 slice frozen butter on each piece. Roll up chicken breasts, tucking under ends. Set aside.
2. Combine bread crumbs, cheese, salt, paprika, and parsley in a small dish.
3. Roll chicken breasts in flour, in beaten egg, and then in crumb-parsley mixture. Sprinkle with browning powder, if desired. Place in a flat 10-inch microwave-safe casserole. Cover with lid. Refrigerate 1 to 24 hours (optional).
4. Microwave, covered, 15 to 18 minutes at MEDIUM HIGH (70%),* or until meat is no longer pink. Let stand

....

*Compacts: Microwave for 15 to 16 minues at HIGH (100%) instead of step #4.

Although butter gives Chicken Kiev its traditional flavor, calorie watchers can substitute 1 teaspoon frozen reduced-calorie margarine for the slice of butter. Serve chicken on a fresh bed of parsley sprigs with a baked potato on the side.

For Chicken Kiev Swiss, add 1 tablespoon grated Swiss cheese with the frozen butter before rolling chicken breasts. Proceed as directed.

Use browning powder (such as Micro Shake) to enhance the color, especially if you use bread crumbs instead of cornflake crumbs.

10 minutes. Serve garnished with fresh parsley on a bed of cooked rice.

Yield: 4 to 6 servings.

· ❄ ·

CHICKEN COLOMBARD

4 to 6 split chicken
  breasts, skins removed
  (approximately 2½ to 3
  pounds)
¼ cup cornflake crumbs
¼ teaspoon pepper
1 teaspoon crushed
  rosemary
2 tablespoons chopped
  onion

½ cup Colombard or
  sauterne wine
3 tablespoons butter or
  margarine
2 tablespoons cornstarch
½ teaspoon salt
¾ cup half-and-half
4-ounce can sliced
  mushrooms, drained

1. Arrange chicken, meaty side up, in a 10-inch flat casserole. Sprinkle with cornflake crumbs, pepper, rosemary, and onion. Pour wine into casserole. Cover with lid or waxed paper.
2. Microwave for 20 to 25 minutes at MEDIUM HIGH (70%), until chicken is tender and no longer pink. Rotate pan twice, if necessary, for even cooking. Set aside.
3. Microwave butter in a 1-quart microwave-safe bowl for 30 seconds at HIGH (100%), until melted. Stir in cornstarch and salt until well blended. Add drippings from chicken, half-and-half, and mushrooms. Blend well.
4. Microwave for 7 to 8 minutes at MEDIUM HIGH (70%), until mixture thickens and begins to boil, stirring twice. Pour over chicken.

5. Microwave, uncovered, for 3 to 4 minutes at MEDIUM HIGH (70%), until heated through. Garnish with fresh parsley, if desired.

Yield: 4 to 6 servings.

———————— · ❇ · ————————

TIPS
· · · · · · · ·

If you use large chicken breasts, increase microwaving time in step #4 to 15 to 20 minutes at MEDIUM HIGH (70%).

CHICKEN FANTASTIQUE

———————— · · · · · ————————

3 pounds cut-up chicken (breast pieces and thighs work best), skins removed

½ cup French or Russian dressing

1 cup apricot jam

1-ounce packet dry onion soup mix

1. Arrange chicken on a microwave baking rack with thickest pieces to the outside of the dish.
2. Mix remaining ingredients to make sauce. Spread over chicken pieces, reserving one-third of the sauce for later basting.
3. Cover with waxed paper. Microwave for 10 minutes at HIGH (100%). Turn each piece over and baste with remaining sauce and drippings. Cover again with waxed paper.
4. Microwave for 10 to 12 minutes at MEDIUM HIGH (70%), or until no longer pink. Let stand, covered, on kitchen counter for 5 to 10 minutes.

Yield: 4 servings.

———————— · ❇ · ————————

· ·

Duty makes us do things well, but love makes us do them beautifully.

SAUCY VENISON ROAST

.... • • • • • ....

.... ROAST ....

2–3 pounds venison roast
Microwave browning
   powder for meat, garlic
   and onion flavored

1 teaspoon Worcestershire
   sauce
3 slices bacon

.... SAUCE ....

2 tablespoons flour
¼ cup cooking wine or red
   wine

4-ounce can sliced
   mushrooms, undrained
1 tablespoon minced onion
   (optional)

1. **Roast:** Sprinkle venison liberally with browning powder and Worcestershire sauce. Place on a bacon rack and cover with waxed paper.
2. Microwave for 10 minutes at HIGH (100%).* Turn meat over. Sprinkle with browning powder. Cover with bacon strips. Microwave again, for 20 to 25 minutes at MEDIUM (50%), or until internal temperature is 160°F. (medium done) to 170°F. (well done). Cover with a casserole lid or foil to retain heat. Transfer drippings and liquid to a 1-quart microwave-safe bowl.
3. **Sauce:** Combine flour and wine in a small microwave-safe dish until smooth. Stir into liquid drippings. Stir in mushrooms and onions. Microwave for 3½ to 4½ minutes at HIGH (100%), until boiling. Serve poured over roast, or on the side.

Yield: 6 to 8 servings.

———— · ❄ · ————

*Compacts: Microwave roast for 12 to 15 minutes per pound at HIGH (100%), total time.

Microwave browning powder (such as Micro Shake) greatly enhances the color of any roast made in the microwave oven.

HOT CHICKEN SALAD
· · · · ·

2½ pounds chicken
  breasts (4–6)*
1 cup hot water
3 large eggs
2 cups diced celery
1 tablespoon chopped
  pimiento (optional)
½ cup slivered almonds

¾ cup (3 ounces) shredded
  American or Cheddar
  cheese
1 cup mayonnaise or salad
  dressing
¼ cup crushed potato
  chips or seasoned bread
  crumbs

For added flavor, dissolve 1 cube chicken-flavored bouillon in the hot water before adding to chicken in step #1.

For Cold Chicken Salad: Cool chicken after slicing in step #1. Substitute ⅔ cup seedless green grape halves, 8-ounce can drained pineapple chunks, and 1 small apple, cored and chopped, for the cheese and 1 cup of the diced celery. Omit potato chips and prepare as directed, omitting microwaving time in step #3. Chill salad and serve on a bed of Romaine or iceberg lettuce.

1. **To cook chicken:** Place chicken breasts and water in a 10-inch flat, microwave-safe casserole. Cover and microwave for 14 to 16 minutes at HIGH (100%), until meat is no longer pink. Let stand 5 minutes. Remove skin and bones. Slice into bite-size pieces. Set aside.

2. **To cook eggs:** Break eggs into 3 custard cups. Prick whites and yolks with a fork twice. Cover with waxed paper. Microwave for 3 to 3½ minutes at MEDIUM (50%), until white is set and yolk is almost set. Let stand 1 minute. Separate yolk from white and set aside.

3. **To make salad:** Chop egg whites. Mix whites with the chicken, celery, pimiento, almonds, and cheese in a greased 2-quart microwave-safe casserole. Mash egg yolks and stir into mayonnaise. Mix mayonnaise mixture with chicken mixture. Top with crushed chips. Microwave for 3 minutes at HIGH (100%). Rotate dish. Microwave for 8 to 10 minutes at MEDIUM (50%), or until heated through.

Yield: 6 to 8 servings.

———— · ❄ · ————

*You can substitute 3 7-ounce cans chicken for the chicken breasts. Omit #1.

POTATOES AND HAM AU GRATIN

(OR SCALLOPED POTATOES VARIATION)

———————— · · · · · ————————

Great for leftover ham or a take-along casserole for potlucks.

½ cup hot water
5 to 6 medium potatoes (2½ pounds), peeled and thinly sliced
4 tablespoons butter or margarine
3 tablespoons flour
1 teaspoon dry mustard
1⅔ cups milk

1 cup (4 ounces) grated sharp Cheddar cheese, divided
Dash of salt and pepper
1½ cups cubed, cooked ham
¼ cup green onions, sliced

1. Pour water over sliced potatoes in a flat 2-quart microwave-safe casserole. Cover with lid. Microwave for 10 minutes at HIGH (100%),* stirring once. Let stand for 5 minutes. Drain. Pour potatoes into another bowl and set aside.

2. In the 2-quart casserole, microwave butter for 20 to 30 seconds at HIGH (100%). Blend in flour and mustard. Stir in milk. Microwave for 2½ to 3 minutes at HIGH (100%). Beat well. Microwave again for 2 to 3 minutes at HIGH (100%), until thickened.

3. Stir in ¾ cup cheese until melted. Stir in potatoes, seasonings, ham, and onion. Microwave for 12 to 15 minutes at MEDIUM HIGH (70%), or until potatoes are tender. Sprinkle with remaining cheese. Microwave again for 1 to 2 minutes at MEDIUM HIGH (70%), until cheese is melted. Let stand 5 minutes.

Yield: 6 to 8 servings.

———————— · ❅ · ————————

*Compacts: Microwave in step #1 for 18 to 20 minutes at HIGH (100%) and in step #3 for 12 to 15 minutes at HIGH (100%).

TIPS
....

For Scalloped Potatoes: Omit cheese. In step #3, sprinkle top with bread crumbs and a dash of paprika instead of the cheese.

For a special cheesy flavor, increase grated sharp Cheddar cheese to 2 cups. Stir 1½ cups cheese into the potatoes in step #3, reserving ½ cup for the topping.

Use a nongeneric brand natural spaghetti sauce. From my experience, generic brands lend a starchy taste to the lasagna.

If you don't have time to refrigerate at least 2 hours: After combining sauce in step #3, microwave sauce mixture for 5 minutes at HIGH (100%), or until very hot. Proceed as directed in step #4 (excluding refrigerating), instead of step #5.

Shield corners and microwave for 20 minutes at MEDIUM HIGH (70%) in step #5. Remove foil shielding. Microwave again for 3 to 5 minutes at MEDIUM HIGH (70%). Let stand 15 minutes.

See page 9 for tips on shielding.

MEATLESS LASAGNA
· · · · ·

No need to precook the noodles.

·············· RICOTTA MIXTURE ···············

10-ounce package frozen, chopped spinach (optional)

2 cups ricotta or drained cottage cheese

1 medium egg

3 tablespoons fresh chopped parsley or 1 tablespoon dried parsley

¼ teaspoon nutmeg

·············· CHEESE MIXTURE ···············

¾ cup Parmesan cheese, grated

3 cups mozzarella cheese, grated

·············· SAUCE ···············

32-ounce jar spaghetti sauce

1 teaspoon Italian seasoning

½ teaspoon basil

1½ teaspoons sugar (or sugar substitute)

¼ cup diced onion

·············· NOODLES ···············

8 ounces lasagna noodles, uncooked (use either white or whole wheat)

1. **Ricotta mixture:** Microwave spinach (optional) in the package, on a paper towel, for 5 to 6 minutes at HIGH (100%). Unwrap and drain well. Combine ricotta cheese, drained cooked spinach, egg, parsley, and nutmeg in a mixing bowl until well blended. Set aside.

2. **Cheese mixture:** Combine Parmesan and mozzarella cheese; set aside.

3. **Sauce:** Combine sauce ingredients; set aside.
4. In a 12 × 8-inch microwave-safe baking dish, layer one-third of the sauce, one-half of the uncooked noodles, one-half of the ricotta mixture, one-half of the cheese mixture. Repeat layers, ending with the sauce. Cover with plastic wrap. Refrigerate 2 to 24 hours.
5. Shield corners with foil. Microwave for 25 minutes at HIGH (100%). Remove foil shielding. Microwave again for 5 to 7 minutes at HIGH (100%). Let stand, covered, on kitchen counter for 5 minutes.

Yield: 6 to 8 servings.

———— · ❄ · ————

INDEX

· ❄ ·

MICROWAVE AIDS
WHAT IS MICRO SHAKE?

Micro Shake is an all-natural seasoning developed solely for microwave cooking. It includes a blend of herbs and spices that beautifully browns, tenderizes, seals in juices, and deliciously seasons meats.

Micro Shake contains *no* MSG, sugar, preservatives, or artificial color yet boasts of only 4 calories per ½ teaspoon.

• Set of three shakers includes: Natural Fish, Country Fried Chicken, and Meat with Onion and Garlic.

• Salt-free (0 sodium) set of three shakers includes: Natural Meat, Country Fried Chicken, and Natural Fish.

WHAT IS A MICROWAVE CANDY THERMOMETER?

A microwave candy thermometer is designed to be left in candy, soups, or casseroles while microwaving and can be easily viewed through the oven door. It registers temperatures to 325°F., which makes recipe conversion from conventional to microwave very easy. The thermometer has a paddle that can be used for stirring and an adjustable clip to hold the thermometer upright in the cooking utensil. This wonderful aid to candy making can be washed in the dishwasher.

HARD-TO-FIND MICROWAVE AIDS

For your convenience and in answer to many requests, Micro Shake and Microwave Candy Thermometers can be ordered using the cookbook order form.

ORDER FORM

· ❄ ·

Additional copies of *Easy Livin' Microwave Cooking for the Holidays* can be ordered directly from the publisher by returning the coupon below with check or money order to St. Martin's Press, 175 Fifth Avenue, New York, N.Y. 10010, ATTN: Cash Sales. For information on credit card orders, quantity orders, and discounts, call the St. Martin's Special Sales Department toll-free at (800) 221-7945. In New York State, call (212) 674-5151.

You may also enjoy *Easy Livin' Microwave Cooking,* a primer designed for beginning microwave cooks, also by Karen Kangas Dwyer.

Please send me _____ copy(ies) of EASY LIVIN'
MICROWAVE COOKING FOR THE HOLIDAYS
(ISBN 0-312-03480-6) @ $10.95 per book $_____

Please send me _____ copy(ies) of EASY LIVIN'
MICROWAVE COOKING (ISBN 0-312-02910-1) @
$10.95 per book $_____

Postage and handling
($1.50 for first copy + $.75 for each additional book) $_____

Amount enclosed $_____

Name _____

Address _____

City _____ State _____ ZIP_____

Any of the products shown on page 252 can be ordered directly from the author by writing: Karen Dwyer, P.O. Box 471, Boystown, Nebraska 68010. Please make check or money order payable to Karen Dwyer.

———— sets Micro Shake (3-shaker set) @ $8.95 $————————

———— sets Salt-free Micro Shake (3-shaker set) @ $8.95 $————————

———— sets Microwave Candy Thermometer(s) @ $7.95 $————————

Postage and Handling charges are included in the above prices.

Amount enclosed $————————

Send to:

Name _____

Address _____

City _____ State _____ ZIP_____

ABOUT THE
AUTHOR

Karen Kangas Dwyer was graduated from the University of Nebraska with a B.S. degree in home economics and a Master's degree in communication. In addition to teaching junior and senior high school home economics for eight years, she has worked as a microwave specialist and instructor for Sharp Microwave Ovens and as a home economist for Litton Microwave Ovens. Karen Dwyer currently gives microwave presentations for television and for community organizations, and teaches public speaking classes at the University of Nebraska at Omaha. She is also the author of *Easy Livin' Microwave Cooking*.